HAUNTED COLUMBUS, GEORGIA

PHANTOMS OF THE FOUNTAIN CITY

FAITH SERAFIN

Faith Serafin

Published by Haunted America
A Division of The History Press
Charleston, SC 29403
www.historypress.net

First published 2012

Manufactured in the United States

ISBN 978.1.60949.552.7

Library of Congress CIP data applied for.

And my soul from out that shadow that lies floating on the floor
Shall be lifted—Nevermore!

—Edgar Allan Poe

CONTENTS

Contents

ACKNOWLEDGEMENTS

I would like to recognize all the people who helped contribute to this book in some way. First and foremost, I would like to thank my family for standing by me and supporting me through another haunted adventure, my friends and team members from the Alabama Paranormal Research Team, who relentlessly and passionately, seek out the legends and ghosts of our communities. I would like to acknowledge Bruce Smith and Susan Ingram from the National Civil War Naval Museum. Bruce and Susan supported my research in the paranormal and its relevance to historical objects and locations. I must give great credit to my dear friends Michelle Smith for her help in critiquing my material, and to Tonya Campos for joining me in endless graveyard scavenger hunts. I'd also like to recognize Dustin Cooper for rekindling my imagination regarding local unsolved mysteries.

I would like to personally thank everyone who obliged me with interviews in and around the community: Lisa Wyrick and Joyce Cathey, P.J. Adams and award-winning Alcatraz historical interpreter Monica Cobis; the staff at the Rankin House; the Ma Rainey House Museum; and Linwood Cemetery. Also, thanks to everyone who made anonymous contributions, including retired Columbus police officers, military and city officials and to those families and people in the Columbus and surrounding communities who shared with me their eyewitness reports and personal accounts from so many of these stories.

Lastly, I must thank all the paranormal enthusiasts, ghost hunters, legend chasers and curious folks who visit my website daily and those of you who attend events and tours hosted by the Alabama Paranormal Research Team. Your support is what keeps me going and drives me to write down the legends of our past for future generations and for all of you who share a passion for the unusual history America has to offer, thank you for lending me your time in an effort to continue my work for future publications of haunted history.

INTRODUCTION

Columbus, Georgia, also known as the Fountain City, holds onto its secrets like the endless flow of the great Chattahoochee River. Its landscape has changed with time and industry, but the spirits of this city speak out from beyond the grave. This area was once home to the Muscogee Creek Indians. They built a great and thriving empire in this region and, throughout their history, spread a verbal legacy of unusual tales, supernatural beings and legendary beasts.

Columbus was named for the Spanish explorer, Christopher Columbus, and because the Chattahoochee River was navigational by sea, it gave way to direct trade routes between Georgia and many parts of Europe. These included England, France and Spain. These European travelers and settlers added diversity to the native society and changed the course of history by adding their own influence on religious and spiritual aspects of the native culture.

Originally a frontier town, Columbus would undergo a dramatic change in less than a few hundred years. Travelers from all over the world would make their way here and bring with them stories and legends of their own. Columbus tells a story in itself, from Indian legends and folklore to famous frontier ghosts and spirits of Civil War heroes. Phantoms of legendary theater houses and some well-known civil rights activists, politicians and even vaudeville performers called Columbus home, and in death, still linger in their former homes, businesses and final resting places.

The preserved architecture of the city is a ghostly and beautiful reminder of the history here. Many original buildings, such as the Springer Opera

House, exist today and are haunted by stories decades old. Magnificent displays of early American ingenuity are proudly displayed up and down Broadway in the buildings, theaters, historical monuments and even New Age art. Everywhere you look there is some sort of history waiting to reach out and grab you.

The hustle and bustle of Columbus, Georgia, echoes throughout history, leaving its mark on those who have lived, worked and died here. Their ghosts call out from beyond the years of historical literature, reaching over oceans of time to resurrect old tales of what once was.

The Ghosts of the Springer Opera House

Columbus, Georgia, has a long and diverse history mixed well into its foundation. These once dusty and dirty streets, riddled with horse-drawn carriages have now given way to automobiles and street lights. The trolley cars of the middle century have long vanished under the sidewalks, but the shadowy presence of an eighteenth-century opera house at 103 Tenth Street still remains.

The Springer Opera House is one of the most spectacular theaters in the South. Its graceful architecture is a beautiful setting of Corinthian columns, heavy aprons, stained glass and a captivating proscenium framed stage. Staircases lead to elaborate balconies overlooking the crowds. Entering the theater arouses an intoxicating mixture of the senses. The sights, smells and even the feel of the old building have a regal appeal that even the simplest folks can truly appreciate.

Francis Joseph Springer was a European immigrant and moved to Columbus before the Civil War. He made his living as a successful grocer and was an avid lover of theater and music. Joseph had a dream to construct a beautiful Victorian theater in Columbus. His contribution and dedication gave birth to the Springer Opera House, which opened on February 21, 1871.

Many wonderful and historical figures have graced the Springer over the last 140 years. Some of the earliest recognized figures include, Edwin Booth, the brother of John Wilkes Booth (who assassinated President Abraham Lincoln). Edwin Booth was a renowned actor of the nineteenth century, performing in Shakespearian plays like *Hamlet*, and he was regarded as one of the greatest actors of his time. James O'Neil, the actor who reluctantly played the leading role in the stage rendition of *The Count of Monte Cristo*, and Charles Sherwood Stratton, known for his performance as *General Tom Thumb*, performed here under P.T. Barnum and what is today known as the Barnum and Bailey Circus.

Oscar Wilde, the famed Irish writer and poet, spent a spell in Columbus. His novel *The Picture of Dorian Gray* portrays Wilde's aestheticism. The novel tells the story of Dorian Gray and his portrait, which ages while Dorian stays young. The story was hailed as a literary masterpiece (along with many of Wilde's other literary works). Wilde himself was a close and dear friend of Lillie Langtry, known as the "Jersey Lily," who performed at the Springer as well. She was a beautiful, British-born woman who was notorious for the many lovers she kept throughout her lifetime. This regal mistress kept the company of many prominent men, such as King Edward VII, English lord Charles Chetwynd-Talbot and Prince Louis of Battenberg, a sea lord and relative to the British Royal Family. Her life was as colorful as her acting career, and it was her talent that led her to the Springer Opera House.

Toward the middle of the nineteenth century, many notable figures would add themselves to the growing entourage of the Springer's celebrity status. Will Rodgers, the Cherokee-born comedian, actor and vaudeville performer of the 1920s and 1930s was one such person. Anges Demille was a dancer and choreographer who graced the stage in ballets. Ethel Barrymore was a New York Broadway star and distant relative of present-day actress Drew Barrymore. Columbus native Gertrude "Ma" Rainey made her debut here at the Springer in a talent show. She would later perform countless minstrels and vaudeville shows all over the United States and abroad. John Philip Sousa, known for the "March King" and who is most recognized for writing "Stars and Stripes Forever," also performed at the Springer.

William Jennings Bryant was a prominent liberal Democrat and political figure. He gave lectures at the Springer. He was also an avid prohibitionist during the Speakeasy era and a dedicated Presbyterian. The thirty-second president of the United States, Franklin D. Roosevelt, was also a Georgia native and gave lectures and speeches at the Springer Opera House in the hopes of motivating the people of his great state through the Great Depression.

These are but a few people who have graced the Opera House with their presence. Today, the Springer has overcome phenomenal odds. Two renovations in the last 140 years have resurrected this vessel of magic and

The Springer Opera House is a stunning eighteenth-century American theatre house.

turned it into a virtual wonderland of historical and supernatural energy. Though time has changed the old building, history has influenced the Springer's ghost stories, and they are among Georgia's most recognized.

While some of the Springer's own employees and even city officials would prefer the Springer Opera House be left out of ghost stories, there are no shortages of experiences in the old theater. Many actors and students who work or perform at the Springer have had at least one other-worldly experience that they can't easily explain away. When weary designers spend days without end, preparing for shows and rummaging through endless racks of costumes, the spirit of the costume room is said to lend a helping hand when asked. Others have seen the entity of a man who mirrors the movements of his would-be victims. Icy vortexes emanate from walls, and items from some rooms must be kept as they are, for if they are moved by any living being, the perspective poltergeist will put them back in there original location.

A couple from New York reported a strange and unnerving experience at the Springer while preparing for a performance. During a play, a husband and wife acting team waited behind the curtain for their stage call. Just as the wife was about to go onto the stage, she turned to her husband and said, "What?" When he replied "what?" as well, she asked, "Did you just tap me on the back?" "No," he said. She was then cued onto the stage, but for the rest of the evening, the woman was very nervous and perplexed as to who had tapped her.

Some of the earliest reports of supernatural activity stem from the early years of the Springer, including one that tells of a young female child who fell to her death from one of the upstairs balconies. Others believe the ghosts of the Springer's long and flamboyant past have somehow come back to this beloved theater to continue their star-bound journeys. Perhaps it's a matter of the heart, allowing the emotions of millions to embrace the old theater like a fragile loved one. Today, the Springer is still holding classic performances, and even a few new ones, with new and aspiring actors and players.

It's possible that many are oblivious to the supernatural power of the Springer Opera House. However, with its history and the magnitude with which it has endured the changing times, it stands as a beacon in the city, an inextinguishable flame loved by all and adored by all others as it hosts performances of the living and nonliving alike.

Port Columbus

Georgia's Most Haunted Museum

Traveling along Alabama Highway 280 toward Columbus, Georgia, a few miles from the rural country areas of southeast Alabama and southwest Georgia, you enter a very different kind of "South." As Victory Drive curls around the mighty Chattahoochee, one is reminded of the Civil War era and the industry that helped build Columbus, Georgia.

At 1002 Victory Drive, part of that history is stored and preserved in a brick structure. The National Civil War Naval Museum-Port Columbus started construction in 1999 and opened for business on March 9, 2001, the 139th Anniversary of the Battle of the Ironclads. The museum's original housing structure was located in a separate location near what is today known as South Commons. In 1962, Governor Earnest Vandiver dedicated the Confederate Naval Museum after the stern portion of the Confederate Ironclad, the CSS *Jackson* (also called the CSS *Muscogee*), was recovered from the Chattahoochee River, and in 1963, the front section of the *Jackson* was also recovered and added to the display.

In 1964, a thirty-foot section of the CSS *Chattahoochee* was also recovered and put on display in the makeshift museum. In 1970, the museum displays were open to the public and more artifacts pertaining to the Confederate navy were added. However, in 1974, the museum was closed due to budget cuts, and by 1985, the museum had been reduced to one employee and was later cut from the city budget all together.

In 1995, the museum was included in a community plan to raise money for a new facility that would include Union and Confederate artifacts alike, and in 1999, construction began on the new building. Port Columbus boasts a variety of Union and Confederate artifacts; most of them have a long history of being passed down by generations of Civil War descendants and collectors. Perhaps the most remarkable artifact at Port Columbus (and perhaps of any remaining Civil War artifact in existence) is that of the CSS *Jackson*.

On December 22, 1864, the CSS *Jackson* was launched at the naval yard, which was located at 600 Front Avenue in Columbus, Georgia, on the banks of the Chattahoochee River. The Confederate ironclad was engineered by Confederate engineer James Warner and was set to aid the Confederate navy in the war. Its thick armor plating and sturdy wooden body was a sight to marvel. It was about 223 feet long and weighed four million pounds upon its completion.

Once the war reached Columbus, it was merely a matter of time before the Union army and James H. Wilson's Raiders would intercept the ships at the navy yard. When Wilson's troops reached Columbus, they set the *Jackson* on fire and sent it down river. It burned for more than two weeks before it finally succumbed to the blaze and burned to the waterline where it sank. The *Jackson* remained in its watery grave for almost one hundred years until it was salvaged and placed in the National Civil War Naval Museum. Though its remaining original exterior is rather harsh, a metal skeleton depicts the size and shape of her original structure. The ship was never involved in battle, nor does it have any gruesome historical significance. However, it does have its fair share of ghostly inhabitants.

Guests at Port Columbus are drawn to the massive structure like moths to a flame, and people have occasionally reported hearing footsteps on the ship. The ship no longer has a deck, and no one is allowed on the artifact. Ghostly whistles like that of a steamship are also heard around the *Jackson*, and the strange moans and voices of men and women are also heard here. These ghostly voices and sounds were captured on digital recorders by the Alabama Paranormal Research Team in August 2009, after ghostly antics finally convinced museum staff to get help from paranormal investigators and to document the phenomenon.

The *Jackson* may be the largest attraction at the museum, but the paranormal activity isn't just centered there. The CSS *Chattahoochee* is a smaller artifact with a more frightening history. The *Chattahoochee* was a more conventional looking ship with mast and steam powered engines, but an unfortunate explosion caused a terrible tragedy aboard this ship. The event took place after an engineer made the mistake of pouring cool water into

"Powder Monkey" was a term used for young men who carried black powder loads for cannons onboard ships during the Civil War.

a hot boiler. The steam engine exploded, ripping through the ship and its crew, decapitating one young man and killing several sailors immediately.

The remaining crew members who made it to shore waited for several days until help finally arrived. For some, it was already too late; many of the survivors had perished awaiting relief. Others died of severe infection of burns and wounds in local hospitals just days after being rescued. The ghostly figure of a decapitated powder monkey roams this area of the museum near the ship's remains. (Powder Monkeys were typically very young boys, often as young as fourteen and fifteen years old, who were commissioned to carry the black powder loads that were placed inside cannons before they were fired, a dangerous job for a youngster, or a man of any age.)

Inside the main galleries, an array of assorted ships' flags are strategically placed along the walls. Many of these flags have seen great battles and were flown among some of the Union and Confederate's greatest ironclads, gunships and blockade runners. Perhaps the flags upon this wall that tell the most horrible stories are that of the CSS *Tennessee* and the USS *Hartford*. The CSS *Tennessee* was built in Selma, Alabama, and launched in February 1863. It was commissioned a year later as Admiral Franklin Buchanan's flagship and set forth to Mobile, where it engaged in what would later be known as one of the Civil War's most spectacular naval battles.

August 5, 1864, marked the Battle of Mobile Bay as Union Admiral David Farragut launched his assault on the Confederate stronghold (Fort Morgan) at Mobile Bay. Hours of intense fighting erupted as the Confederate fleets fought diligently to withstand the Union. As Farragut entered the bay aboard his flagship, the USS *Hartford*, a submerged mine was struck by a smaller gunship just ahead of the fleet. Farragut was signaled of the ship's attack and that torpedoes were in the shallows within the bay. Farragut promptly replied, "Damn the torpedoes, full speed ahead!" coining one of the greatest military slogans of all times.

During the intense battle, the Confederate fleet withstood hours of heavy gunfire and cannons, devastating the Confederate Navy. The ironclad CSS *Tennessee* held its ground and waged the battle but finally succumbed to the Union—but not before a horrible fate would take one engineer's life by surprise.

During the battle, a gun port on the Tennessee was lodged in the open position. An engineer was called down to unhinge the bolt, or to loosen the gun port, so it could be closed. The engineer was leaning against the interior of the ship to gain an advantage over the rusty bolt. He reached above his head and placed a large wrench over the bolt and began to tug. Suddenly, a four-hundred-pound cannonball slammed into the side of the ironclad. The engineer was instantly liquefied from the waste up. A report on the incident claimed that his remains had to be mopped up with a bucket and thrown overboard. Today, the flags of these ships remain secluded and silent, encased in glass and protected from the elements inside Port Columbus. It leaves one to wonder what the flags would say if they could talk.

Other artifacts inside the museum consist of a blood stained surgeon's coat worn by John Luck, who was a surgeon and prisoner of war held captive by the Confederate army at Battery Wagner near Charleston, South Carolina. He was held for a year, even though a truce was ordered that pertained to enlisted men. The Confederate army dismissed the order and kept Luck because he was an officer. Luck tended to countless victims of the war, Union and Confederate alike; however, he is the reason the story of Union Colonel Robert Shaw and the Fifty-Fourth Massachusetts is known today.

Colonel Shaw led a regiment of black troops during the Civil War. More than two hundred of his beloved Fifty-Fourth were killed at Battery Wagner along with Shaw. Shaw was shot through the heart and died almost instantly during battle and was buried with his troops in a mass grave. When the order from Shaw's family came down to recover his body, the Confederate officers in charge denied the request as an insult, stating, "Not for a man who [led] black troops." The story, however, lives on largely in part because of John Luck and his time spent as a captive at Battery Wagner.

Inside the replicas of the museum, the USS *Hartford* and the CSS *Albemarle*, strange phenomenon seems to breathe life into these mock wonders. While no original pieces of either the *Hartford* or the *Albemarle* are part of the mock up, spirits tend to find refuge from the living inside them. The replica of the USS *Hartford* is built as an example of how enlisted sailors and officers would have lived aboard a ship. Walking inside the *Hartford* seems harmless enough; however, one ghostly gentleman seems to think the *Hartford* is his own personal portal between the living and the dead. He has been seen quite frequently thumbing through maps and even walking through walls in and around the seafaring replica.

Perhaps he is looking for a crew or maybe just preparing for what is soon to be another nautical battle. Regardless, he is not very friendly and museum staff and guests can attest to that. Former staff member Susan Ingram has seen the man in the *Hartford* and stays clear of the area as much as she can. Other staff members and former employees have stated the same, and one visitor at the museum reported that she entered the *Hartford* one afternoon and approached the wardroom of the cabin and was met by a man in a blue uniform looking through what appeared to be maps. When her eyes met his, he promptly looked at her and gave her the thumb as if gesturing to get out. In addition to this sighting inside the *Hartford*, Deborah Funk, a Phenix City native, was on a Sea Ghost Tour in October 2009 when she was pushed by an unseen force while exiting the *Hartford*.

Other peculiar circumstances inside the museum seem to be most concentrated in the room where the replica of the *Albemarle* is located. The full-scale reproduction of the town along the Albemarle Sound in North Carolina takes a visitor back in time and depicts what a port town would have looked like during the Civil War, complete with the Confederate ironclad *Albemarle* docked at port. The room also tells the story of Lieutenant William Cushing, also known as "Lincoln's Commando." His heroic achievements during the Civil War gained him wide respect for his bravery and semi-insane methods of fulfilling his orders.

Cushing was a force to be reckoned with. His insatiable appetite for glory was short-lived but a major contribution to the Union forces. His plan to sink the *Albemarle* may have been as mad as he was, but it worked. Cushing planned to intercept a small steamship and go up river. Gaining a full head

A replica of the CSS *Albemarle* is on display at the National Civil War Naval Museum.

of steam, he would then turn the ship around and head back down river toward the *Albemarle* at full speed. His plan was to stick the *Albemarle* with a spar torpedo, which is essentially a bomb on a stick.

A large log boom made of large trees and chains surrounded the Confederate ironclad and Cushing intended to jump the boom with his small steam vessel and jam the spar in her side. And on a dark and chilly October night, he did just that. Cushing had slipped past the Confederates long enough to get within just a few feet of the *Albemarle*, when a dog on the bank began to bark and alerted Confederate troops. The steam vessel Cushing was on jumped the slimy log boom around the *Albemarle* and the spar torpedo was launched into her hull. The explosion threw the sailors from both ships. Most of Cushing's men swam safely to shore, but they were later captured. Cushing escaped, swam to shore and, later, was safe behind Union lines.

Though the story of William Cushing is extravagant, the room that holds his history is also as bold and notorious for supernatural phenomenon. This room has produced some of the strongest paranormal evidence ever witnessed by paranormal investigators. In late 2010, the Alabama Paranormal Research Team was filming for a production based on its paranormal investigations at Port Columbus. During this time, director

Faith Serafin witnessed a strange grunting sound that came from inside the mock up room of Albemarle Sound. Suddenly, a glowing pair of white eyes began to emanate from the darkness, like that of an animal in the headlights of a car. It walked just past the walk way that leads onto the ship and suddenly disappeared.

During the same night, paranormal investigator Brandon Stoker also witnessed a strange white mist that appeared in the form of a man. It walked in his direction and then turned around and disappeared within a few seconds. Both of these experiences were captured on film by the team and stand as some of its most credible evidence to this day. Museum staff members Helen Vinson and Danielle Ribolini have also reported seeing the strange white mist in the museum near the *Albemarle*. Could it be Lieutenant Cushing's ghost making his presence known in his typically brazen way?

Many questions continue to bring about unanswered phenomenon inside Port Columbus, and in April 2012, the television show *My Ghost Story* contacted the Alabama Paranormal Research Team about paranormal experiences to be featured in an episode of this nationally recognized television show. Even today, flying books launch themselves from shelves inside the museum gift shop, strange voices from beyond the grave reverberate inside the hollow walls and ghostly structures create a home for the Civil War undead. And still, more and more reports continue to pile into the museum day in and day out about its ghostly inhabitants. You may find yourself at Port Columbus for a little educational tour but remember to stay on your guard, or you might be the next patron to be shanghaied by the ghostly crew of Georgia's most haunted museum, the National Civil War Naval Museum.

The Mother of the Blues

The "Ma" Rainey House

Gertrude Pridgett was born April 26, 1886, in Columbus, Georgia. She grew up in a very poor family, as many African Americans did in that time. In 1897, Gertrude received her education at the Fifth Avenue School for African Americans, one of the first black schools in Muscogee County. Her parents, Thomas and Ella Pridgett, both from Alabama, and her grandmother were singers. At a very young age, Gertrude started to show signs of talent. She started performing at the age of fourteen in talent shows and at local theaters. In 1900, Gertrude Pridgett debuted at the Springer Opera House in the Bunch of Blackberries Talent Show, which would serve as a critical starting point to her lavish and colorful vaudeville career.

In 1904, Gertrude married William "Pa" Rainey, who was also an artist and comedian. Shortly after her marriage in 1917, she began to travel in minstrel and vaudeville shows, where they were known as "Madame Gertrude Rainey and her Georgia Smart Sets." She performed all over the South, in the Midwest and even in Mexico. She marveled her audiences with her flare and flashy attire; her shiny, flapper dresses were stitched with red sequins and reflected her boisterous personality. She usually accented her wardrobe with a headband of beautiful feathers, embroidered with the image of an eagle (which was also featured in backdrops during her stage performances). She carried a plume of fancy ostrich feathers and wore long dangly earrings, necklaces of gold and large strands of pearls that added to her capped, gold-tooth display of what a professional jazz musician of the era would look like.

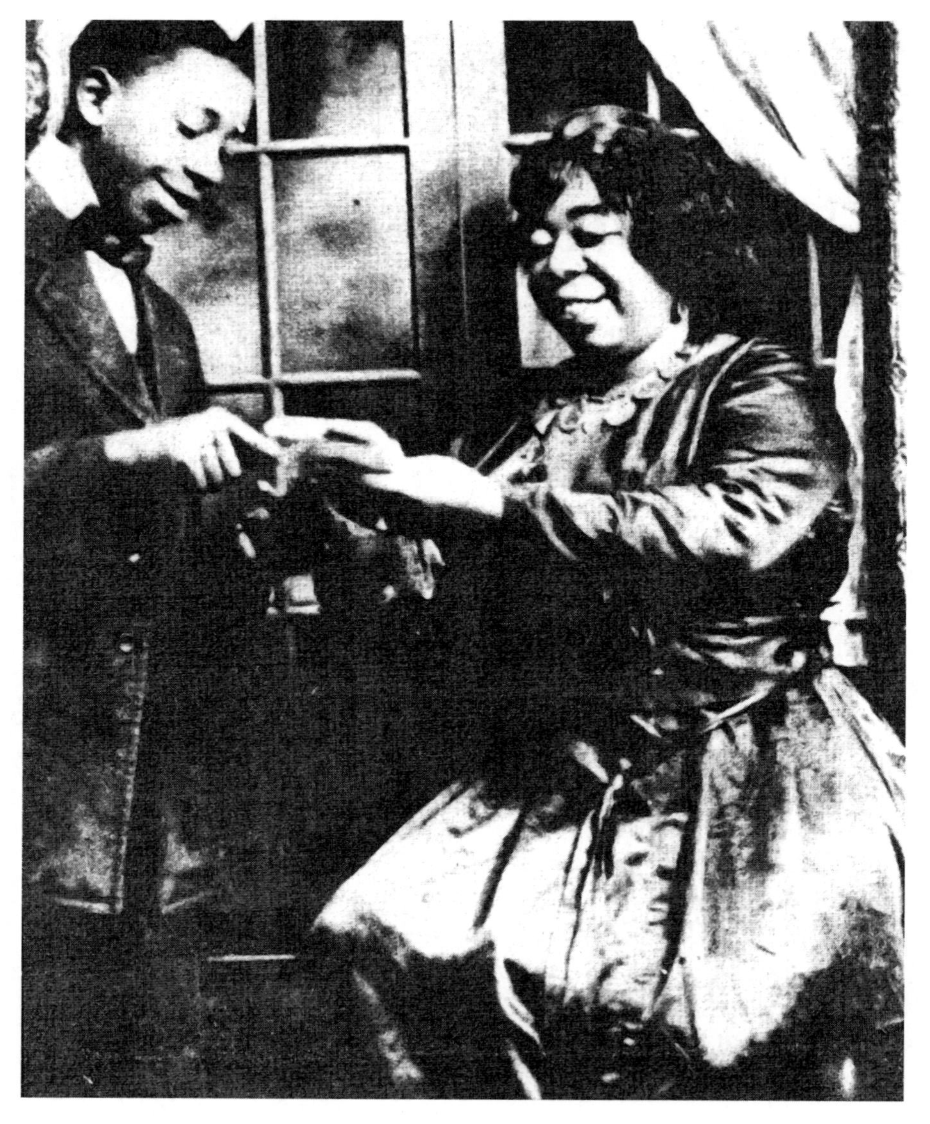

Gertrude "Ma" Rainey with one of her fellow vaudeville performers. *Courtesy of the Columbus Library.*

Jazz musicians during this time were a very influential part of American music, and with black artists struggling to make their place in primarily "white" America, particularly in the South, jazz music was evolving into a great movement. In the early years of slavery, blacks were seldom allowed to communicate with each other and used song as a means of speaking to one another. It also helped motivate them through long, hard workdays.

Though song had long been a traditional part of African religion, celebrations and work, many white slave owners deemed this type of communication "devil's music," since most white Christians were prohibited from singing and dancing by their own religions. However, with the emancipation of slavery, many black performers found work in the entertainment industry.

With the evolution of African American music came variations of traditional folk and gospel music, later giving way to forms of instrumental and vocal diversity, such as swing, ragtime, and later, jazz and blues. No one really knows the true origins of the jazz music known as the blues, but it is understood that this type of music was intertwined with African American slavery and serves as a legacy of the hardships and the progress of blacks in America.

Ma Rainey was a pioneer in the industry of jazz and blues. Dubbed "Mother of the Blues," she recorded her first albums with Paramount records in Chicago in 1923 and spent the next seventeen years touring with shows like the Georgia Wildcats Band. While on tour, she met Thomas Dorsey, the famed "Father of Black Gospel Music," who influenced future musicians like Elvis Presley and Johnny Cash. She also toured with the Louisiana Blackbirds Revue in 1927. She recorded another album for Paramount in 1928 with the Tub Jug Washboard Band and several other artists. In 1930, she toured with the Arkansas Swift Foot Revue until 1933, when she began to tour with the Al Gaines Carnival Show.

Ma Rainey influenced and worked with many jazz musicians of her time, including Bessie Smith, often called "The Empress of the Blues," who toured with Ma and Pa Rainey for several years. Ma Rainey also worked alongside Mamie Smith, "The Queen of the Blues," and Willie Mae (known as "Big MaMa") Thornton who was the first to record "Hound Dog" and "Ball and Chain," both of which were later rerecorded by Elvis Presley and Janis Joplin. Ma Rainey also recorded "Jelly Bean Blues" with famous New Orleans native Louis Armstrong.

Ma Rainey recorded nearly one hundred songs during that era, and during this time, black artists had the freedom to express emotions and tell a story within their music. The song "Black Eye Blues" tells of domestic abuse, while "Black Bottom" refers to the dance craze that originated in New Orleans. The song "Bo-Weavil Blues" may perhaps reflect on her separation to her estranged husband, William "Pa" Rainey, whom she was separated from but never divorced. "Moonshine Blues" tells of a distraught woman who is perhaps realizing she is dying and wants to go home. And in 1935, Ma Rainey did just that.

After more than a decade of touring and recording some of America's most fundamental music, Ma Rainey returned to Columbus, Georgia. She lived at what is today 805 Fifth Avenue in Columbus. Though she struggled to salvage her career through the Great Depression, she still managed to foster seven children but never had any of her own. She also managed the Liberty Theatre in Columbus, Georgia, and another in Rome, Georgia.

On December 22, 1939, Gertrude "Ma" Rainey died at the age of fifty-three in her Columbus home from heart failure. Her funeral was held at the Friendship Baptist Church where she sang in the choir after her retirement from the vaudeville circuits. She was survived by her siblings, including her brother Thomas Pridgett, whose name is still visible in the cement sidewalk in front of the Ma Rainey Home today. There are some arguments to whether or not her brother may have been slightly jealous of her fame, since he indicated she was nothing more than a "housekeeper" on her death certificate.

Housekeeper or not, Ma Rainey has left her mark on the world of music. Years after her death, in 1983, she was inducted into the Blues Foundation Hall of Fame, The Jazz Hall of Fame, The Rock and Roll Hall of Fame (1990), The Georgia Music Hall of Fame and The Grammy Hall of Fame (2004). The United States Post Office also featured Ma Rainey on the twenty-nine cent commemorative postage stamp in 1994.

Throughout the years, the Ma Rainey House has undergone extensive reconstruction to breathe life into what is now a living museum. The home includes some original pieces, like Ma Rainey's piano, which has been restored and now sits at the farthest point of the entrance hallway, a portrait painting hangs in her downstairs bedroom and even some of her original recordings on vinyl records have been collected by the museum. Traveling show posters like one reading "Rabbit Foot Minstrels," and articles of achievement are displayed elegantly against the plaster walls of Ma Rainey's former home.

Though Ma Rainey spent most of her living years traveling the vaudeville circuits all over the United States, in death, some believe she may still be taking up residence in the old Rainey home. Her body rests in the Porterdale Cemetery, located along Victory Drive in Columbus, but her ghost has been reported to have been seen and heard at the Ma Rainey Home. Employees and visitors of the Rainey home and museum have reported strange and unusual phenomenon for years. Though it's not very frequent, even a few curious occasions are enough to unnerve the biggest skeptic.

On one particular day, two friends and possible descendants of the Rainey family ventured to the house for a tour. Both women were highly superstitious and would not even walk past the stairway for fear of a rumored murder that took place up stairs. According to the two women, a story had been handed down in their family of a man who was shot and killed upstairs in the Rainey home many years ago. Though no evidence of the murder has ever been found, the pair would not dare go upstairs even when invited.

Other visitors of the Ma Rainey House and Museum have reported hearing the sound of piano music while visiting, although Ma Rainey's music is played on a CD inside the home. When asked, the woman who reported to have heard the piano said, "I was standing right next to it, and it was as if someone had run a hand through the keys." On occasion, patrons who pass the home have seen a black woman dressed in a funny hat dancing on the upper level balcony.

An employee at the museum stated that she was walking through the house once and heard a woman's voice come from the top of the stairs. "Hello?" it called. She said that she went to investigate the voice, and though she searched the entire home, she found no one. She also reported that no further strange phenomenon occurred in the house for roughly a year until one afternoon, when she heard a gurgling sound. She searched the house to determine the source of the odd sound and found the faucet in the upstairs bathroom had been turned on. Later, she witnessed a shade in the downstairs window raise itself without being touched.

People have also reported seeing the ghost of a young African American boy in the home, possibly between the ages of five and eight. He is typically reported as having very short hair (he was possibly bald), wearing denim overhauls and being barefoot. Could he be the culprit in the shade shenanigans? Or might he be at fault for leaving the bathroom water running as most children do? Or could it be Ma Rainey still dancing the Black Bottom atop her balcony cabaret? Visitors who come to the Ma Rainey house should know that her home and her life may be Columbus's best kept secret but not on purpose.

With so many instrumental African American people in the world of jazz music from the Jim Crow era, it seems Ma is still trying to make her place among them. Still dancing the night away with her sweet, speakeasy spunk and pouring out her soul in every jazzy tune. So listen well when at the Rainey residence: You just may catch a breeze or two, and perhaps if you're lucky, the voice of the "Mother of the Blues."

LINWOOD CEMETERY

Linwood Cemetery is the oldest cemetery in Columbus, Georgia. In 1828, the highest spot on the northeast part of town was surveyed and set aside as the town's cemetery. For the better part of a hundred years, the residents of Columbus were buried here, and a few still own plots today. The cemetery is a twenty-eight-acre location and the final resting place of some of Columbus's most historical and influential people. Grand monuments carved by stonecutters of the past and cast-iron fences serve as a haunting reminder of the craftsmanship and dedication people had for the resting places of the dead.

The history of the cemetery and its dead are a mixture of religious, military, political, scientific, artisan, literary and entrepreneur backgrounds. In 1852, a section of the cemetery on the west end was purchased and is now known as the Jewish Section. The markers and tablets that mark this section are, at first glance, very similar to the common markers and tablets throughout the cemetery. However, upon looking more closely at these particular markers, Hebrew text can be found inscribed on the back. Some are prayers and others are simple dedications to the person buried.

A tinsmith named Louis Haiman, whose Jewish lineage stemmed from Prussia in Europe, and his brother, Elias, settled in Columbus prior to the Civil War. They built a successful industry in sword making and founded the Confederacy's largest sword making company. Haiman's Sword Factory was once located on what is today First Avenue in Columbus, Georgia. The factory manufactured weapons to include the Colt Navy Pistol, Bayonets, swords and farming equipment. Though the factory was burned by Union forces in April 1865, Haiman continued to manufacture farming equipment for Columbus and Atlanta after the war ended. Louis Haiman's grave marker is inscribed with traditional Hebrew text and is among the most recognized in the Linwood Cemetery Jewish section.

Just north of the Jewish section and also on the east end of the cemetery is the resting place of the Confederate dead. One prominent military figure also buried here (but not among this particular section) is General Henry Lewis Benning. Fort Benning, called the "home of the infantry" and located just south of Columbus, is named after General Benning, who was perhaps most noted for his actions during the Civil War. His involvement and dedication during the battle of Antietam, also known as the Battle of Sharpsburg, where he held a bridge during the battle for several hours and repeatedly drove back attempts to overtake the location by Union Forces, earned him a substantial reputation.

Benning also led his men at the Battle of Gettysburg in Pennsylvania, where he charged furiously into battle at Devil's Den, one of the most gruesome battles of the Civil War. He later fought under General James Longstreet at the battle of Chickamauga, only to have his horse shot out from underneath him twice. He was finally successful once he relieved an artilleryman of his horse and rode it into battle without a saddle. Benning also practiced law in Columbus after the war until his death in July 1875.

Colonel John A. Jones was the brother in law of Henry Benning and was killed at the Battle of Devil's Den at Gettysburg. Colonel Jones has a memorial at Linwood Cemetery, but his final resting place is at sea. After his son Leonard traveled to Gettysburg to retrieve his father's remains, the ship carrying his body met a foul storm. Leonard was rescued, but his father's body was swept out to sea, lost forever.

James Warner is also buried at Linwood. He was the chief engineer in the building of the CSS *Jackson*. The *Jackson* was a Confederate ironclad constructed in Columbus at the navy shipyard, which was once located on the banks of the Chattahoochee River. This ship never saw battle but was set on fire and burned into the river. The remains of the ship were rescued in 1963 and are now on display at the National Civil War Naval Museum, located on Victory Drive in Columbus, Georgia.

Not far from James Warner, just to the southeast, lies Noble Leslie DeVotie. He was born in Tuscaloosa, Alabama, and organized the Sigma Alpha Epsilon fraternity at the University of Alabama. He was a pastor during the Civil War and at the First Baptist Church of Columbus. His grave is marked with an elaborate monument dedicated to him by the fraternity he organized and for his selfless dedication to his faith and education.

In the oldest part of the cemetery, just under an enormous and majestic oak, you will find the grave of a very important woman named Lizzie Rutherford. Lizzie Rutherford was born June 1, 1833, and died in Columbus on March 31, 1873. She was a member of the Columbus Soldiers Aid Society, an organization dedicated to helping soldiers after war and also preserving gravesites of those who died during the Civil War. Rutherford organized and founded the first Confederate Memorial Day. Typically held in April for most southern states, the event is organized by different chapters of the United Sons & Daughters of the Confederacy each year and is still celebrated today.

Perhaps the most interesting war related figure buried here is that of William Dudley Chipley, who was arrested for his alleged connection to the murder of George Washington Ashburn. Ashburn was an appointed judge in Columbus who supported the abolishment of slavery prior to the war. Ashburn lived among the slaves and was considered a scalawag among his fellow southerners. On March 28, 1868, Ashburn was murdered by a group of men who disguised themselves in hoods. Many believe these men were affiliated with the Ku Klux Klan. William Chipley was arrested along with several other prominent people from the community. His trial would make national headlines after he was set free when Georgia ratified the Fourteenth Amendment, which was not in motion prior to Chipley's trial. Chipley's case has been a sour conspiracy for decades in Columbus.

The graves of Revolutionary War soldiers George Wells Foster, who moved to Columbus after 1836, and Reverend James Allen are also among the military graves. James Allen owned a large plantation just across the river in Russell County, Alabama, and also practiced medicine. The grave of Major Thomas Manduit Nelson, who was the grandson of Thomas Nelson, a governor from Virginia, is also among these military graves. Thomas Nelson also served with several infantry regiments from Virginia during the War of 1812 and, later, became a representative of the fourteenth and fifteenth Congress.

Other political and military oriented people who are buried at Linwood Cemetery are Peyton Colquitt, who dabbled in politics and law before the outbreak of the Civil War. Later, he would also lead the Muscogee Volunteers to Virginia and gain the rank of Colonel with the Forty-Sixth Georgia Regiment. Colquitt fought at Chickamauga where he was killed. Another political figure resting here is James Johnson, who was appointed

Linwood Cemetery is the oldest cemetery in Columbus and is the final resting place of many historical people from the area.

Georgia's twenty-eighth provisional governor by Confederate president Andrew Jackson. The Johnson plot is simple and unmarked. Five unmarked, brick slabs represent the final resting place of James Johnson and his family.

Prominent scientists like John Pemberton, born July 8, 1831, in Georgia, can also be found among the Linwood elite. He invented the formula for Coca-Cola and also manufactured other chemical compounds in his laboratory, like hair dye and perfume. He also made chemicals for photographic development. Francis Xavier Profumo was born in Italy in 1837 but immigrated to Columbus, where he owned and operated a confectionary store known for having the town's best ice cream.

Several Irish-born stonecutters have monuments on display in Linwood, and many of these craftsmen are also buried here as well. John Madden was a local stonecutter who worked with Patrick Adams, a brickmason in Columbus and owner of a well-established brickyard. Works by both can be seen not only in the monuments of Linwood but in other locations around Columbus that included the Racine Hotel, which was demolished in 1944.

Mirabeau Buonaparte Lamar grew up in Milledgeville, Georgia, but later moved to Columbus after he married Tabitha Jordan and started the first newspaper in Columbus, the *Columbus Enquirer*. He was also an avid poet, and after the death of his wife and suicide of his brother, he moved west into Texas where he was later appointed the second president of the Republic of Texas. He is known as the "Father of Texas Education." Mirabeau's wife Tabitha is buried in Linwood. An obelisk marks her grave.

Helen Augusta Howard founded the Woman's Suffrage Association in Georgia, a chapter of the American Woman Suffrage Association. In 1859, Augusta Howard met with Susan B. Anthony, one of America's most influential women during the political movement for women's rights. Augusta's marker reads "martyred," which represents her choice to stand up for her rights as a human being under God.

W.C. Bradley is among some of the other entrepreneurs resting here. Bradley came to Columbus as a cotton farmer when he was only nineteen years old and quickly established himself as a successful businessman in several aspects, which included wholesale industry, ironworks, textiles and banking. He even served as chairman of Coca-Cola until his death in 1947. Joseph E. Webster also established himself in Columbus when he was only fourteen and was later involved in local politics. He was appointed tax assessor, and in 1854, he ran the city's loading dock. The city wharf as it was called was an active location for shipping goods in and out of Columbus on the Chattahoochee River. Joseph Webster and his wife ran the wharf for ten years.

Abraham Illges was a fundamental part of the financial foundation for many early industries in Columbus. Some of these industries included several textile mills to include the Golden Foundry Mill, the Swift Spinning Mill, Lummus Cotton Gin Company and the Muscogee Manufacturing Company. He also helped to enterprise Columbus Electric and Power, Columbus Ice Company, Georgia Midland and Gulf Railroad, among many others. Abraham and his wife, Mary Lou Barnett Illges, are buried together in Linwood.

Those named here are just a few of Linwood's celebrities. Rows upon rows of graves in Linwood mark the final resting places of historical figures. Most people who visit the cemetery today come for the history of the location. The Historic Linwood Foundation hosts yearly rambles in October with players and descendants who dress and characterize the dead and bring to life the people who were once such an influential part of the Columbus community. While there is officially no documentation to any supernatural significance at Linwood, the cemetery serves as a reminder that just because a place has history doesn't necessarily mean that it is haunted.

The Linwood Cemetery has more to offer those who would like to reach back in time to see what life was like in the infancy of Columbus. It rests quietly and is still just beyond the river, its aging face marked with the marble slabs of time. Linwood has overcome many obstacles and stands as a monumental cornerstone in Columbus history. It may be without ghosts and ghouls, but its history is haunting enough.

CARNIVAL GHOSTS

Every October, the leaves begin their vibrant transformation into shades of orange, yellow and red. A sense of excitement begins to fill the crisp, cool, autumn air in Columbus and a fall tradition attracts people and families from all over the surrounding areas when the Greater Columbus Fair arrives in South Commons. The fair has been a Columbus tradition for generations of people who flock to the week-long event for rides, food, sideshows, games and more. On those cool evenings, shouts of laughter echo from whizzing and chugging rides. A rainbow of electric lights turn the heads of every man, woman and child who pass by. Wide smiles of anticipation radiate across the faces of would-be game winners, and the smell of funnel cake and cotton candy invades the nostrils. Even the musk of livestock seems to mingle together until all manner of human senses are excited and focused on an evening of great fun.

Each year, the fair is carried into town on rigs pulled by heavy diesel trucks in caravans. Workers set up each week in different towns all over the United States. The fair we know today is very different from the carnivals and traveling shows of a hundred years ago. In the early nineteenth century, many traveling circuses, carnivals and other shows were brought in on trains and required many cars to transport performers, animals, rides and supplies. Because the railways were a primary source of transportation during this time, there were many areas located along rail system routes for people to travel by to see the carnival.

The Greater Columbus Fair brings an exciting atmosphere to the region every fall as well as the spirits of the 1915 train wreck.

The majority of early carnivals consisted of performing attractions like acrobats, simple magic sideshows, minstrels and vaudeville performers, animals, the strange and unusual "freak show," and later, rides like the Ferris wheel and carousels. Though the early traveling carnival was somewhat glorified, especially in rural America, life as a traveling performer was difficult and the exploitation of people with genetic mutations or physical disabilities was looked down on by most of mainstream society. However, many people with these abnormalities found work in the traveling carnival as a way to provide for their families.

On November 22, 1915, the Con T. Kennedy circus train left Macon, Georgia, and headed for its next stop. A separate passenger train left a nearby station close to Buena Vista, Georgia, too early and met the circus train head-on near Macon Road, six and a half miles outside of Columbus. The two trains collided causing serious damage to the circus train. Upon impact, it was reported that the circus train literally looked like a kaleidoscope as the impact forced the adjoining cars into one another, which caused a massive explosion and killed several people and possibly animals. A few passengers were thrown several hundred feet from the train, essentially saving their lives. The passenger train was also badly damaged but without casualties.

While reports of deaths vary from six people to fifteen, no solid number was determined; most of those unfortunate passengers were burned to mere ashes. A curious item was discovered while investigating the wreckage of the circus train—a human torso of what was believed to have been a man. However, it was later discovered that the torso belonged to a woman who may have been disguised as a man.

The train wreck of 1915 was a historical event for Columbus and one that would not be forgotten. A monument was erected by the Con T. Kennedy Show in Riverdale Cemetery, located on Victory Drive in Columbus. The monument is made of beautiful white marble and carved in the shape of a circus tent. It is said to have been built on the ashes of those taken from the wreckage to commemorate those lives lost on that terrible day.

Most of today's fair goers in Columbus are oblivious to the 1915 wreck, but on several occasions, ghosts of the tragedy make their way back to the fairgrounds in October. Drones of spectators marvel at the festive atmosphere, and the spirits take flight and mix among the living. In the early 1990s, one Columbus woman reported suddenly feeling as if she and her six-year-old son were not alone at the top of the Ferris wheel they were riding. Other people have reported feeling a similar presence on the Ferris wheel, and there have even been reports of a ghostly couple dressed in early nineteenth-century clothing seen in the unoccupied carts.

In the later hours, visitors to the fair have seen men dressed strangely out of fashion and tending to the livestock. Others report seeing the lingering spirit of a young man who stops fair goers and asks for a nickel to ride the train. Strange indeed since nothing at today's fair could be purchased with a nickel, especially a train ride. While reports spill out of the Greater Columbus Fair, other reports of the floating torso are an established story. Believed to be the ghostly apparition of the torso found in the wreckage, this limbless, headless, floating specter has been seen wandering locations near the old Bull Creek Bridge close to Macon Road in Columbus.

According to legend, the torso manifests on those chilly October nights when the fair is in town and wanders aimlessly around where the wreck took place. Since the torso has no head, legs or arms, it is understood that this limbless ghost can't find its way to the fair and is destined to stay a residual entity, forever seeking its destination.

It seems the magnitude of such a terrible tragedy has damned some souls to an eternity of wandering. It's not known whether these fiendish fair ghosts are the souls of those lost in the train wreck or perhaps the ghosts of fair lovers who have simply found their way back to what they loved in life. The magic of the fair and carnival shows is something special that seems to take hold of the living, engraving itself in our hearts and in our memories, wielding its mystical power and captivating souls.

THE LIVING LIGHT IN GEORGIA

THE WYRICK FAMILY HAUNTING

Now the Spirit speaketh expressly, that in latter times shall depart from the faith, giving heed to seducing spirits and doctrines of devils.
—1 Timothy 4:1

The biblical verse above acknowledges the existence of communication with the dead. It also acknowledges the existence of evil in the realm of the living and how human beings are affected by the spirits of those long dead. This is the case for one such Georgia family who fought to save their daughter from the realm of the dead for more than fifteen years.

The Wyrick family was a normal, young family just starting out in Ellerslie, Georgia, located just a few miles from Columbus. The family first admired the little house on Swint Loop when their daughter, Heidi, was only four. They later purchased the home in the small quiet community. It was a rural community located in the Georgia countryside, and the majority of people living there were retired or elderly.

Heidi had no brothers or sisters at the time and spent long days with her mother, Lisa, at home. Though she was an only child, she didn't seem to mind and had a wonderful imagination that kept her company. She played in the front yard of their new home and often found comfort in being outside. Though Lisa kept a watchful eye on Heidi, she could not foresee the influence of the spirit world that flocked to Heidi on a daily basis.

Over time, Heidi would confide in her mother about the new friend, Mr. Gordy, whom she had made friends with at the new house. She told her

The grave of James Gordy, located in Park Hill Cemetery. He was the supernatural playmate of Heidi Wyrick for many years.

mother that Mr. Gordy was an old man, with white hair and a black suit. He always wore the same black shoes. He was playful and often pushed Heidi on the swing near the back of the property. While Lisa initially thought Mr. Gordy was a living person who sought ill will against her daughter, she quickly learned that Heidi had other "friends": A young man named "Con," who wore a bloody T-shirt and had his hand wrapped in a bandage, and a darker figure she could not identify.

Heidi had indicated early on that her "friends" were of a realm that not all could see. She played with Mr. Gordy for years; he even took a part in helping her learn to ride her bike. Even though most of her family dismissed her ramblings of Mr. Gordy and Con as her playful and highly intelligent imagination, they were very real to Heidi. So real, in fact, that she had more encounters with the spirits of the dead over the years in the Swint Loop house; they seemed to flock to her as if she were a lighthouse in the middle of some dark, dead ocean.

Heidi witnessed many months of paranormal phenomenon, and shortly after, her family began to take a very real interest in her reports of the spirits. Heidi's aunt, Joyce Cathey, bought the property next door to the Wyricks' home and moved in with her two children. On one particular day, the former owner of the property stopped by to give Joyce some documents. The documents consisted of years of deeds of former owners and that of the history of the area which was owned by the former owner's family since 1914.

Joyce thumbed through the documents and came upon an old deed with the signature "James Gordy." Joyce was quick to ask the former owner who James Gordy was. She proceeded to tell her that James was a realtor for a long time in the area and handled the estate of her mother. He was also a well-loved member of the community and an active member of a local church. He drove the church bus that picked up local children and was also involved in church functions like sports among others. When Joyce asked where James Gordy lived, her heart nearly sank when her guest told her that he had been dead for nearly thirty years.

Joyce relayed this information to Lisa and informed her that James Gordy had been dead for a very long time. Lisa was dumbfounded and struggled to understand. Could this be the same Mr. Gordy that Heidi spoke of so frequently? Was he the man in the black suit whose shoes were always the same? A bundle of emotions took over Lisa and Joyce, and for the next several weeks, they spent countless hours researching the Gordy family history.

Although Mr. Gordy had seemed like a harmless entity, Lisa awoke one night to Heidi standing at her bedside with long, deep, bloody claw marks on her cheek. Not long after, Andy, Heidi's father would have a similar experience when he awoke to similar scratches on his torso. It seemed as if whatever was affecting Heidi was now taking out its evil agenda on the entire family.

Heidi had never mentioned to her mother or father that Mr. Gordy was malevolent, nor did she give them any impression that his spirit could have been the one who inflicted the scratches on Heidi and Andy. But it was soon discovered that Heidi could attract both good spirits, and unfortunately, evil spirits and that these relentless entities would be to blame for the countless attacks on the family while at the Wyrick home.

Not long after Heidi was scratched, the family contacted a noted parapsychologist from the University of West Georgia. Dr. William Roll had been studying the paranormal since the early 1950s. He took a particular interest in Heidi and her family and worked closely with a team of scientists and the Wyrick family to find a scientific reason as to why Heidi was able to see and communicate with spirits.

Heidi was only a child and didn't understand a lot of the scientific aspects of the investigation being conducted, but to her, Mr. Gordy was very real and soon she would show her family and Dr. Roll just how real he was. Dr. Roll acquired an old photograph of Mr. Gordy and placed it in a stack of other photos. Dr. Roll handed the stack of photos to Heidi and asked her if she could find the picture of Mr. Gordy. Without hesitation, Heidi flipped through the photos and had properly identified James Gordy's photo as the same man who had been her playmate for so many years.

Though Heidi's family was astounded by her ability to identify the photograph of a man who had been dead for thirty years, to Heidi, he was just as real as anyone else. During this same time, a similar experiment with photographs would reveal that the spirit Heidi called "Con" was indeed a man who lived near the Wyrick home and had also passed away many years before Heidi was even born. He was a relative of the former owner of Joyce's property whose name was actually "Lon," but the fact that he had his hand cut off in a cotton gin accident less than a block from the house in Ellerslie was enough to convince the Wyricks that Heidi did indeed have a sixth sense and an extraordinary ability to see the dead.

Heidi's years came and went, and by the time she was in high school, she had faced some of the worst ridicule of her life. Though neither she nor her family had intended to exploit her abilities, once her story was made public and hit national television, Heidi was a sensation in the paranormal community; however, she faced enormous odds in the world of skeptics, and while some people believed and loved her, others were cruel and hateful.

Heidi was the product of many generations of women and men who had an uncanny ability to see, hear and even communicate with the world of the dead. Heidi's grandmother grew up in a location in Gainesville, Georgia, known as Haunted Hollow. For generations, people lived in the region they called "Hainted Holler," and for many years, strange and unusual phenomenon had been reported in the area.

In the early 1800s, miners flocked to the Gainesville area because of its rich gold deposits. Though the area was still known as Indian Territory, it didn't stop early frontier people from traveling to North Georgia from as far away as California. The potential to "strike it rich" was worth the migration, even with hostile Indians occupying the area. Haunted Hollow or "Hainted Holler" was said to be haunted by the spirits of disgruntled Indians forced from their land, and it is possible the land had been cursed by the natives.

Heidi's grandparents both reported that they also had seen similar apparitions of spirits throughout their lives, and Lisa was no different. When Lisa was a child, she also had a series of sightings similar to her daughter's, but most were now just foggy memories. However, watching Heidi grow up with the ability to see the dead was a fine line between a gift and a curse. Though Heidi felt abandoned by her peers as a young woman, she found refuge in her family and in her faith. When asked how her family has dealt with the years of paranormal phenomenon, Lisa stated, "You just have to believe in them."

Mr. Gordy would soon fade away from Heidi's sight, but the old man who had kept her company for so many years was always with her. Heidi has endured years of dealing with psychic abilities not by her choosing. However, with generations of loving, caring people to support her, she has grown into a woman of spectacular nature, a beautiful and humble child of God. She no longer fears the ability of what is often referred to as "sight," nor does she face the ridicule of skeptics alone.

There will always be skeptics and nonbelievers, but that doesn't keep the Wyrick family from staying strong and advocating for others with similar abilities like Heidi. Today, Heidi is a happily married mother of beautiful twins. She still lives in the west Georgia area but keeps her distance from the house on Swint Loop. The Wyrick family continues to stay clear of the old house. Whether or not Heidi was able to see the spirits of the old house in Ellerslie by nature or science doesn't matter; the fact is that her case of supernatural phenomenon is well documented and could be one of the most elaborate paranormal cases of the twentieth century in southwest Georgia.

BLIND TOM

WHERE IS THE GHOST OF THOMAS WIGGINS?

Charity Wiggins was a slave woman who belonged to Wiley Jones, a cotton plantation owner in Muscogee County, Georgia. She was known as a woman of "good breeding" and was reported to have had as many as twenty-five children in her lifetime. Charity and her children lived an extraordinarily hard life as slaves. The cotton plantation she worked on was large, and Mr. Jones had many slaves. Wiley Jones was not a man of compassion and held little respect for the human lives, working his slaves like livestock on the plantation.

On May 25, 1849, at the age of forty-eight, Charity Wiggins gave birth to a son. What should have been a joyous day of celebration was a day of panic and fear for Charity. Just minutes after the birth of her son, Charity held her baby and looked at him. She counted his fingers and toes, looked at each tiny wrinkle in his newborn skin and softly stroked his tiny head. Every inch of him appeared to be normal, but when she looked into his eyes, she saw that her precious baby's eyes were far from normal. His eyes, which should have been hazel, were instead a misty grayish and almost white color. Her newborn was blind.

Charity had worked in the Jones' house for many years, and she knew that her master would not be happy taking on the burden of a handicapped slave. In this time, it was not uncommon for disabled slaves, adult or child, to be murdered at the hand of a disgruntled taskmaster. Charity knew her son's life was hanging by a thread.

Charity quickly handed the baby to Valeria Jones, the seventeen-year-old daughter of Wiley Jones, and announced that Valeria would have the privilege of naming her infant son. Charity silently hoped that this strategic move would spare her newborn's life and that Valeria would bond with the infant. Valeria was flattered by Charity's request and named the infant Thomas.

Over the next several months, Charity made a very dedicated effort to keep Tom away from Wiley Jones. She feared everyday might be Tom's last. Over time, Charity was paired with another slave, owned by a neighboring plantation owner named Miles Greene. A field hand named Mingo was to be Charity's new husband. Little is known about Mingo except that it is possible that he came from the area of the Dominican Republic and that his ancestors were brought to the Americas by white slave traders. This culture in the Caribbean has a deeply rooted Voodoo religion (known as Santeria in Cuba), which some cultures still practice today. This mixture of African tribal folklore and West African deities were mingled into Catholic beliefs after the Spanish brought Christianity to the Caribbean on trade and slave routes.

Older slaves during this time still had very strong ties to their native religions. Tom was blind, which essentially caused the discoloration of his eyes, but to the medicine men and Voodoo women of the slave community, Tom was a very special and uniquely gifted child. They believed that he had a gift of clairvoyance, which meant he was able to communicate with the dead as well as with deities. Tom was sought after later in life by those believing he had the power to communicate with the dead for séances. This was not uncommon in the slave community, and though Charity wanted to believe that Tom was unique, she still feared for his safety.

In 1850, Wiley Jones found himself in serious debt. He placed an article in a local paper to auction off some of his servants and field workers. Charity and Mingo feared they would be separated by the auction since Mr. Jones made no effort to keep slave families together. He was more interested in how much monetary gain was involved, even if it meant that Charity, Mingo and their children were all sold off separately.

In late December, Charity sought out a respected lawyer and newspaperman from Columbus, Georgia. General James Bethune was born and raised in Georgia and gained a substantial military reputation in the Indian Wars of 1828. After his military service, he attended the University of Georgia, where he studied law. He later moved to Columbus. When Charity and Mingo flagged down General Bethune on a cold December day, Charity pleaded with him to purchase her family at auction, but Charity's pleas were not met with the compassion she had hoped for.

General Bethune was a businessman and had no use for farm hands since he did not have fields that needed planting nor cotton to be picked. James Bethune had house servants but not as many as a working plantation. A few days after Charity pleaded with Bethune to save her family, her prayers were answered. He came to the Jones Plantation and purchased Charity and her entire family. When Bethune arrived home with the new slave family, his wife shouted to him in frustration, "We already have more than I can take care of!" Though the Bethune family may have had reservations about bringing in another slave family, it wasn't long until James Bethune would realize how much of an investment he had made in doing so.

For the first few years of Tom's life, he displayed very unusual and unpredictable behavior. Despite his blindness, he was prone to running off from his mother and siblings in charge of tending to him. In his toddler years, he was considered a bit of a nuisance, and a wooden box was constructed to keep Tom confined so that Charity and her family could work. Tom would spend hours in the box with no stimuli other than sound. His inability to learn like other children earned him the label of a moronic child with no sense or perception or reality, but his small body housed an enormous spirit that would evolve into a twisted fate for both Tom's and the Bethune family.

When Tom reached age three, he began to have even more elaborate tantrums and other unusual episodes of mocking sounds and even people. Though the slave community was notorious for folklore to deter children from straying away from home, the tales of Bloody Bones, Ole Raw Head, boo-Daddies and haints did not have much of an impact on Tom. His over stimulated sense of sound drove him to endure the unassuming dangers of his sightless world. He was frequently found outside at night humming and mocking animal sounds. Tom also had a tendency to inflict pain on unsuspecting family members—not out of anger or malice but because the sound of a shouting sibling seemed to excite him. This was also the case with music.

The Bethune family was lively in the sense that every Bethune child, three boys and four girls, played a musical instrument. One afternoon, the Bethune sisters were in the music room of the Bethune home. As they sat together singing a song, they noticed that a separate voice seemed to emanate from the chorus. The strange voice sang in all variations, from alto to soprano. The sisters were surprised to see Tom just outside the window lying on his back. He seemed to peer into the air, as if only he could see the song floating out the window. Surprised at the accuracy and enthusiasm of Tom's actions, the Bethune sisters quickly brought him inside the house and into the music room.

The girls showed a genuine love of Tom's ability to reproduce a sound, and shortly after, James Bethune bought a piano. The striking sound of the piano seemed to conjure Tom almost instantly. His emotional connection to music connected his very soul to every key played. Tom again became quite a nuisance in his determination to get inside the house to the piano. He was repeatedly caught hammering away on the instrument, his milky white eyes glaring into a world that was only his, a world of stimulation through sound and music.

Tom's earliest moments with music would set in motion a lifetime of musical servitude. Tom may have been born into slavery, but he had no idea what it meant to be a slave or even have a color. The only color he knew came from the beauty and joyful sounds that bellowed from the piano inside the Bethune house. Tom's ability to repeat and memorize was remarkable. He would twist himself into strange contortions when listening to a tune and would clap and laugh out loud, but once the music stopped, he became upset. He even approached Fannie Bethune on one occasion after she stopped playing a tune on the piano. Tom physically pushed her from the seat and then sat at the piano and played the exact tune perfectly.

Tom was no longer considered the poor, blind slave boy who, from birth, was considered a burden. He slowly found a place in the Bethunes' home and was treated much better than the average slave. Tom's abilities to repeat sound accurately and precisely are characteristics of children with Autism. However, in the days of slavery in America, there was no diagnosis or treatment for children or adults with these types of mental disabilities, and Tom was simply considered ignorant and with no more sense than the family dog, but his uncanny ability to duplicate sounds and music made him an enigma.

General Bethune quickly noticed that Tom's unusual gift had the potential to gain hefty revenue. By age five, Tom had conceived his first musical composition, *The Rain Storm*. This piano piece consisted of accurate interpretations of the sound of rain as it trickled and softly fell to the ground, and even thunder and lightening all seemed to be channeled through Tom and manifested as music as he played the piano in his strange and unusual trance. General Bethune was a businessman and he would soon thrust himself and Tom into a lifetime of traveling musical shows.

Tom began to tour with James Bethune as early as age five (some reports say he was eight). Tom didn't seem to mind. His insatiable compulsion to play music was inevitable, and James Bethune was reported to have made millions of dollars parading Tom all over the United States and Europe.

Cyclone Galop, composed by Thomas Wiggins, is among many musical compositions written by the enslaved musical savant.

James Bethune was a big contributor and supporter of the Confederate army, and on the heels of the Civil War, Tom wrote a new composition, *The Battle of Manassas.* Tom would travel from town to town, and proceeds from shows were used to help the Confederate cause. General Bethune even denied the audiences of Union states for fear that abolitionists would steal Tom from him.

Even though Tom was indeed a blind black savant during the slave era, he led a very comfortable life. Many people who have studied Thomas Wiggins's life will argue that he was nothing more than a cash cow to the Bethune family, but others will say he was indeed a very well kept man. His condition kept him separated from emotional ties to people, but his simple-mindedness was sometimes more a burden to the puppeteer rather than the puppet. Tom was given a small share of money he earned to spend, but money had no meaning to Tom. To Charity, however, the extra money earned through Tom was an enormous comfort to her and her family.

Charity Wiggins lived to be one hundred years old, and even in her one-hundredth year, she could recall all her children and most of her grandchildren. But throughout her lifetime, she longed for Tom to be with her. In the state of slavery, she was in no position to request her child be returned to her. So Tom spent many, long years traveling away from his family. Thomas grew into a fine gentleman, and though he was still traveling extensively with the aging James Bethune, Charity was all but a fragment of a memory to Tom.

Throughout Tom's life, numerous articles were written by several authors, and these would contribute to the legacy of the "blind prodigy." Mark Twain wrote, "Some archangel, cast out of upper Heaven like another Satan, inhabits this coarse casket; and he comforts himself and makes his prison beautiful with thoughts and dreams and memories of another time... It is not Blind Tom that does these wonderful things and plays this wonderful music—it is the other party."

The world around Tom was truly a terrible place. He had no idea that the war was causing economic hardships throughout the entire South, nor did Tom know that he was a free man under the Emancipation Proclamation. James Bethune took care of every avenue to keep Tom comfortable, but he also took advantage of Tom, and Charity paid the ultimate price as his mother, being essentially erased from his fragile mind. Tom Wiggins was a true musical genius beyond his time, despite his ignorance and childlike mind. And he did show signs of mental breakdown and stress-related illness throughout most of his adult life. Most of these episodes resulted from the lengthy custody issue that kept the Bethune family and Charity Wiggins locked in a battle over Tom.

The great Harry Houdini even took a crack at Tom, calling him a "psychic fraud," though Tom had no more understanding of what it meant to be a fraud as opposed to a magician. Tom's understanding of such controversy was void. His simple genius was awkward but astonishing. On the other hand, his own people saw him as a supernatural figure, a being of great strength and power, with the gift of sight not of this world. Without the proper ability to verbally or emotionally communicate, Thomas Wiggins was able to display his emotions through the music he played. Many believe Blind Tom had a gift to see the world through sound. To feel a world through touch could only come as a last resort, but not for Tom. This was Tom's world, and though his music may be recognized today, so can the legends associated with him.

In the summer of 1908, while in Hoboken, New Jersey, Tom was struck with illness, suffering what many believe to have been a stroke. He sat at the piano when suddenly he slumped over. Shortly thereafter he again went to the piano and started to play, but when he placed his right hand to the keys, he said, "Tom's fingers won't play." Tom passed away soon after. According to official records, he died June 13, 1908, and was buried in Brooklyn, New York, in Evergreens Cemetery. But prior to his death, for the better part of three years, strange reports of his death began to circulate. One report read that Tom had perished in the Johnstown flood in Pennsylvania in 1889; another said he died of consumption; and another said that Tom had jumped from the Eads Bridge in St. Louis, Missouri, while on tour there.

Today, most of the rumors have been laid to rest about the tragedies that seemed to circulate in regards to Tom. However, there is a larger debate that still exists today. Tom died in Hoboken, New Jersey, where he lived with Eliza Bethune, his guardian at the time. Eliza evaded authorities for years after Tom was emancipated. She became a recluse and avoided contact with everyone except her nephew. After Tom's death, Eliza arranged to have him buried in Brooklyn, New York. But Charity Wiggins, who had not been able to see or know her son, was determined to have his body sent back to Columbus. Fannie Bethune advocated having Tom's body sent back to the Bethune plantation. It's rumored that she was successful in doing so and that Tom's remains were brought back to Columbus and placed in the Bethune family plot just adjacent to the home.

Today, two markers lay claim to his gravesite, one in Brooklyn, New York, at the Evergreens Cemetery and the other in Columbus, Georgia, at the

Blind Tom, age ten, was deemed an ignorant child but was, in fact, a musical genius. *Courtesy of the Columbus Library.*

Westmoreland estate. Tom's body may be at rest in either New York or Georgia, but his spirit is still as uneasy in death as it was in life. Tom's nature was unusual due to his mental condition, and his ghost may be just as unusual. Rumors are occasionally heard in Columbus about the Westmoreland estate, where Tom was supposedly reburied. If Tom is buried here, his spirit must still be in the state of a five-year-old child.

On foggy nights, travelers on the Warm Springs Road often report seeing a very young boy dressed in a long white shirt. He seems to wander aimlessly in the dark and vanish into the surrounding forest. One Columbus native confided that she had approached the Westmoreland estate just before dark. The location was gated and locked. She proceeded to put her car in reverse and back down the driveway, and when she turned again to look in front of her, there stood a small African American child in what she said looked to be an old-fashioned nightgown. He looked up at the sky and hummed an eerie tune. She shouted to him to please go home since it was nearly dark. He then sat down on the pavement just inside the gate. As she watched the strange boy for a few seconds, she noticed that he seemed to be crying.

She looked down to put her 1982 Buick in park and then reached for the door handle to open the driver's side. As she stepped out of her car to comfort the crying child, she looked at the gate where he had been standing. The boy was gone. She called out for a few minutes and listened to hear if he had run away. Though she was genuinely concerned at the time, she could not locate the boy and called the local sheriff's department to report the incident. The search turned up nothing, and it wasn't until years later that she realized that she may have witnessed the ghost of Thomas Wiggins.

Other stories are told of the same boy climbing on the gates or up into surrounding trees on the estate, always humming or singing a ghostly tune. The apartment area where Tom once shared housing with Eliza Bethune Lerche in Hoboken, New Jersey, is also rumored to have some unusual activity. The area is now part of the historical district in Hoboken, but some say that Tom's spirit is still hard at work, channeling the ecstasy of music through the spirit world. For decades after Tom's death, residents of the apartments reported hearing Tom's piano play, sometimes at all hours of the night. Inhabitants of the apartments have never found this supernatural occurrence anything more than a nuisance, and it's believed today that Tom is still playing his ghostly serenades.

Whether Thomas Green Wiggins still haunts the Westmoreland house or the historical district in Hoboken, New Jersey, is only for us to speculate. What we do know about Tom is that his circumstances and unusual disability led him to many places in the world that most people will never see. Sightless and mindless to his surroundings, he lived his life in a world of musical bliss. Tom was oblivious to the evil of the world and eternally a child of marvelous and monumental ability.

Lovers' Leap

The name Chattahoochee comes from the creek words "chatta," meaning rock, and "hoochee," which is interpreted as river (or river of painted rock). Near the banks of this magnificent, rocky river, close to where the Highland Dam and remains of the old Bibb Mill are situated, there were once great rapids that spilled over a lofty cliff of granite rock formations. This area once drove the Bibb Mill turbines that spun cotton in the mills for many years. Today, the mill is abandoned and lifeless, but the mighty Chattahoochee still flows with the vigor and stamina of a great locomotive.

Before the mill was built, the area was virgin terrain with massive water oaks and tall pines. Shrubbery and wildflowers grew and fragrant displays perfumed the river air. This was the site of Lovers' Leap, one of Columbus's oldest Native American folklores. Called "Tumbling Falls" by the *Eas-to-cha-ta* (Creek for "Red Man"), history tells us that the neighboring tribes of the Coweta and Cusseta Indians share a legend of a tragic love story that took place here.

The daughter of the aging Cusseta chief was a prize among her people. It's said her beauty couldn't compare to any star in the sky, and she was revered as an almost spirit-like being. Her grace and charm wooed the hearts of anyone who was with her. At an early age, her father called her "Minechee," which roughly translates to overactive and intelligent. She was truly treasured by the chief and was his only daughter. His sons had all perished, and she was the only child left. Minechee grew into a lovely young woman, and she catered to her aging father. In time, he began to call her

The area of the Chattahoochee River known as Lovers' Leap.

"Morning Star," and her name would reflect the beautiful maiden in perfect harmony as she grew.

In the neighboring Coweta town, the son of the chief Young Eagle had fallen deeply in love with Morning Star. They met secretly at first. Young Eagle would use his *cohamoteker,* or blow gun, to signal Morning Star by rolling a piece of magnolia into a tight ring and shooting it at her feet. She would follow his secret messages until they could meet in solitude. Young Eagle was prepared to take Morning Star as his mate, but hostile tendencies broke out between the neighboring tribes and divided not just the villages but Young Eagle and Morning Star as well.

Soon after, a child was born to the maiden, and the baby was presented to the Cusseta chief. Though the arrival of a baby was joyous, bad blood still fueled the hostilities between tribes. Morning Star and Young Eagle were separated for some time due to the feud. During this time a jealous and ambitious brave named Yaho Hadjo, or "Crazy Wolf," was determined to turn Morning Star's heart, but his jealously toward Young Eagle would cost him dearly in the end.

The villages continued to wage war on one another, and the conflict was fueled by elaborate lies told by Crazy Wolf to the Cusseta chief. His determination to gain Morning Star as a mate would come at any cost.

The aging Cusseta chief was particularly fond of Crazy Wolf, and gifts of prepared venison and other delights were frequently brought to the chief by Morning Star. Though the gifts came from Morning Star's one true love, Young Eagle, the old chief assumed that Crazy Wolf had brought them, and Crazy Wolf made no effort to tell him any different.

After weeks of not seeing his Indian princess, Young Eagle set out to find her and arrange a private meeting. Morning Star was tending a basket of corn when the sweet smell of a magnolia bloom caught her senses. Suddenly, a soft, white petal fell at her feet, and she knew her lover had come to see her. Excited and anxious, she gathered her basket and headed straight for the designated spot where she knew Young Eagle would be waiting, but she had no idea the jealous Yaho Hadjo was quietly following her.

Morning Star met her Young Eagle with open arms, throwing her basket to the ground to embrace him. The pair held each other with great passion as Crazy Wolf looked on from his hiding place in the forest. He then quickly and quietly slipped into the darkness and made his way back to the Cusseta village where he spun a lie to the old chief. He told the chief that he had overheard Young Eagle say that he intended to lead a raid on the unsuspecting Coweta village. The old chief angrily rose to his feet and ordered that Crazy Wolf go wake the sleeping warriors and set out to find and kill Young Eagle. Crazy Wolf asked the chief if he would reward him with the one prize he wanted most, Morning Star. The chief agreed, and the band of Indians set out to find Young Eagle.

Crazy Wolf knew right where to find them, and he anticipated that his plan would be fool proof. Morning Star and Young Eagle were completely oblivious to the diabolical plan hatched by the Crazy Wolf and had no idea what was about to unfold. The warriors reached the secret location where Morning Star and Young Eagle met. Quickly, they ran closer and closer to the couple, and when they reached the cliff trail, Crazy Wolf let out a war cry and raised his tomahawk and ran straight for Young Eagle in an attempt to strike him.

For a second, the attackers stopped as Morning Star flung herself in front of Young Eagle, clinching her arms around him like the talons of a great bird. Young Eagle instantly gathered his lover, and in that one desperate second, the pair ran swiftly onto the cliff trail overlooking the raging Chattahoochee River. They ran for several minutes, and the distance between the angry mob and the lovers grew farther. Young Eagle stopped only for a second, thinking his Morning Star could be spared if he left her behind. Suddenly, the blade of Crazy Wolf's tomahawk met Young Eagle, and in that moment,

Morning Star grasped her lover as he tried to shield her from the attack. A sudden slip on the damp, muddy trail sent the lovers over the cliffs and into the surging river below. The momentum of Crazy Wolf's assault jolted him forward, and he, too, was flung into the swirling depths. The remaining warriors lowered their weapons and looked over onto the sharp granite rocks below where the motionless couple still clung onto their lifeless bodies. Crazy Wolf was swept away by the river. His body was not found.

The warriors returned to the Cusseta village where the chief was waiting to see the scalped body of Young Eagle. Instead, his warriors came to him with heavy hearts. The old chief asked them where his daughter was and about the body of Young Eagle. A lone warrior spoke up, answering, "Great Spirit has taken your daughter and Young Eagle. The jealous Crazy Wolf was swept away by the great serpent and dragged down into his cave."

The chief was riddled with guilt and despair. His one beloved Morning Star was gone and because he had not the heart to stop the feuding between villages, he was now without her and his sons. The chief fell into a great state of depression and he went to the place where his daughter flung herself onto the rocks. For many days, the old chief would not leave. His warriors brought him food and water, but he did not eat. Finally, the warriors brought their chief home, but his body was cold and lifeless, for he too, was now with the Great Spirit.

Today, the location known as Lovers' Leap is still haunted by the two lovers. Occasionally, there is a whirlpool spotted in that area. It is believed that this effect is a representation of the lovers spiraling to their deaths in the cold waters below the cliff. Others say that the whirlpool's spinning motion represents the never-ending love the two shared, suggesting that the lovers are still together even in death.

Columbus Stockade Blues

In 1825, Houston County was the only county with a set of laws in the Creek territory near modern-day Columbus. In late 1825, after the treaty of Indian Springs, jurisdictions were laid out in the area just north of the old county line. That area spanned a distance from the Chattahoochee to the Flint Rivers and became Muscogee County.

Prior to 1858, a structure was erected and deemed the Muscogee County Jail. It was considered a state-of-the-art facility for that particular time period. Records indicate that it was used as the police headquarters as late as 1895, but reports span back as far as 1837 on the inmates who were jailed here. In October 1837, the notorious Creek Indian chief, Jim Henry, was housed during his arrest and trial for crimes against the State of Georgia. He was responsible for leading several raids, massacres and uprisings throughout Georgia and Alabama, including the Massacre of Roanoke and the Battle at Sheppard's Plantation in Stewart County.

In April 1905, a Sheriff shot and killed a suspected bootlegger and was arrested and housed in the jail for murder. He was tried and found not guilty and was later released. An unfortunate chain of events lead to the murder of a twelve-year-old Columbus boy named Cedron Land in 1912. His killer, fourteen-year-old T.Z. Cotton, was a neighbor and was charged with manslaughter after Cedron's body was found shot through the left eye. T.Z. was convicted and sentenced to four years in the state penitentiary. However, before bailiffs could remove him after his trial, several members of the Land family formed a mob and overtook the bailiffs and kidnapped the boy. The members of the Land family then hijacked a railcar that took them to the edge of town, taking T.Z. with them as their hostage. The angry mob then shot T.Z. to death.

The last legal hanging execution took place in Columbus after Gervis Bloodworth and Willie Jones were convicted of a murder that took place in Taylor County. On December 3, 1923, the two men shot and killed a salesman from Potterville, Georgia, in a robbery. The murder of Howard Underwood came as a surprise to the community since he was a successful salesman, husband and father of nine children. Gervis and Willie were said to have robbed Mr. Underwood at gun point before they shot him in the back of the head and left him for dead. Later, they admitted to being under the influence of alcohol. They were arrested, tried and then sent to the Columbus Stockade where they were executed by hanging in May 1925. Gervis Bloodworth and Willie Jones are buried in the same plot in the Girard Cemetery located in Phenix City, Alabama.

In November 1927, a bluegrass duo from Columbus wrote the song "Columbus Stockade Blues." Tom Darby and Jimmie Tarlton met in Columbus and started playing together shortly after. Tarlton and Darby were both banjo players and wrote and recorded more then sixty songs together. "Columbus Stockade Blues" was allegedly written about Tom Darby's brother, who was a sailor and who spent a fair amount of time in the stockade. The bluegrass duo played together for several years and are known for other recordings such as "Birmingham Jail," "The Weaver's Blues" and "Down in Florida on a Hog," just to name a few.

"Columbus Stockade Blues" was recorded in Atlanta sometime after 1927, and its popularity spread throughout the entire United States. It reportedly sold an undisclosed number of copies, but Tarlton and Darby only profited $150 from the song after they sold the rights along with the recording. Since its release, an infinite number of country and bluegrass artists have performed the song, including Johnny Cash, Willie Nelson, Roy Clark, Marty Robbins and even the Grateful Dead. Other artists who have rerecorded Tarlton and Darby's music include Huddie William Ledbetter, also known as the jazz artist "Lead Belly."

In August 1934, the old stockade began to have trouble with overcrowding and fell into a poor state of disrepair. The facility still held inmates but in substandard conditions until December 1972, when it was deemed a fire hazard. Renovations began thereafter, and in 1981, the facility was reopened and housed the overflow from the newly erected jail. Though the stockade's structure has withstood time, its inmates have not. Most of the early Columbus population housed here were poor whites and blacks, men and women alike, who were charged with petty crimes.

"Last night as I lay sleeping/ Oh, I dreamed it was you in my arms/ When I woke I was mistaken/ Lord, I was still behind these bars."

The old stockade has some colorful history and throughout the years stories with similar circumstances have surfaced. As the old song goes, "Way down in Columbus Georgia, Lord I wish I was back in Tennessee, My friends have all turned their backs on me." It just so happened that a lonely, perhaps heartbroken, spirit of a half-drunken old man still frequents this old building. Former deputies of the Muscogee County sheriff's office and even city police officers have reported seeing the old man for many years.

It's said that the old timer is a sad sight indeed, dressed in ragged denim overalls with heavy unlaced boots. This white-haired specter staggers down the narrow corridors in an endless effort to reach an unknown destination. From time to time, a frightful report will come to light about a disgruntled man who shouts obscenities in an angry effort to scare any of the would-be officers or inmates that happen to disturb him in his cell. Some Columbus residents and former officers of the law have said that unusual lights have also been seen in the windows of the stockade at night.

One Muscogee county deputy, now retired, confirmed a report that he had seen an unusual light inside the building while on his way to work in the late evening hours in the summer of 1990. He approached the building and saw a pale yellow light through one of the windows. At first, he thought that the light was perhaps a flashlight from a maintenance engineer. Upon his arrival, he told two fellow deputies about what he had seen, and the three went out to the stockade to investigate the strange light. Since no maintenance personnel were scheduled to be in the stockade, the three men entered the building cautiously. According to the report, an unusual odor seemed to permeate the facility. While some smells were typical (such as dust and moldy odors of the ancient brick structure), this particular smell was very stout, like that of a decaying animal. As the deputies continued their walk through, they branched off alone to patrol the building, expecting to find a dead bird or rodent responsible for the smell.

Suddenly, one of the deputies stumbled in an effort to escape some strange force that seemed to be engulfing him. He shouted out, "Help, he's got me!" and as the other officers made their way to him, they discovered their friend pressed up against a cell, as if someone or something was pulling him inside. The two officers struggled to free their fellow deputy, and as they pursued the invisible assailant, they realized that there was not a soul in the cell. After a brief struggle to understand what had just transpired, the trio agreed that they would not speak of what had taken place to anyone, for fear they would be teased or ridiculed.

Other reports associated with the unusual light say that the old Muscogee County Stockade is haunted by a former sheriff who travels the building at night by lantern light. This seems to correspond with a few old reports handed down by former inmates, who frequented the facility on weekends when they had a little too much to drink. Some say they have seen the ghostly figure of a man holding a lit lantern, and others report just seeing the unusual apparition of a floating lantern, lit up with a pale yellow candle.

Because the building is used as the prison laundry today, the inmates who find themselves lucky enough to work laundry may find themselves scared out of their wits should the invisible force take hold of one of them or the strange ghost lantern shine upon their terrified faces or if they catch a glimpse of the old drunkard who can't seem to find his way. Tarlton and Darby wrote a verse about heartbreak as part of the "Columbus Stockade Blues":

Last night as I lay sleeping
Oh, I dreamed it was you in my arms
When I woke I was mistaken
Lord, I was still behind these bars

Is it possible these souls are trapped in the Stockade? After all, it was meant to keep people in.

The Naval Yard and the Ghost of James Warner

The Columbus Convention and Trade Center is located at 801 Front Avenue in Columbus. It's an impressive brick and iron structure indicative of the time when Columbus was at the peek of the industrial age. It's situated on the banks of the Chattahoochee River, and the railroad tracks run along the side and behind the water front facility. To view the building from the outside, one would assume it was a simple parking garage with some elaborate decor on the outer face, but a view of the inside of the building gives one a better idea of what this old structure was once part of and what it was used for.

Prior to 1860, many of Columbus's mills were located on the banks of the Chattahoochee River to allow for better production and trade due to the riverboat landings. These mills spanned several blocks and even several miles along the river. The Iron Works had established itself as an iron casting foundry and made everything from farm equipment and steamship engines to stoves and decorative iron pieces. By 1862, the Iron Works and textile mills had focused on aiding the war effort and Confederate cause. The Iron Works then began manufacturing guns, swords, mortars and cannons.

In June that year, the Confederate navy leased the Iron Works and began construction of some of the Navy's most elaborate gunships. James H. Warner was a former United States navy engineer who spearheaded the navy yard operations in collaboration with the Iron Works to aid the Confederacy, turning the industry into the largest manufacturer of Confederate machinery in the South. Warner oversaw the engineering efforts of the navy yard in building the Confederate ironclad ship, the CSS *Jackson*,

Confederate engineer James Warner's grave, located in Linwood Cemetery.

as well as the Confederate gunship, the CSS *Chattahoochee*. Both vessels were expected to be major contributions to the Confederate military.

Though the war progressed outside of Columbus, the patriotic community rallied to support the Confederacy. On April 9, 1865, Confederate General Robert E. Lee surrendered to Union General Ulysses S. Grant at the Appomattox courthouse in Virginia. Unfortunately for Columbus, the news of Lee's surrender had not yet found its way to the area, and on the night of April 16, 1865, Wilson's raiders tore through Alabama and into Georgia and destroyed the navy yard and the textile mills located on the river.

Columbus was virtually unprotected due to short supply of manpower, and there was no way to stop the Union forces as they laid waste to the unguarded city. Wilson's raiders quickly took over the navy yard and set fire to it. The Iron Works was salvaged after the raid and rebuilt the following year. More industry was developed under James Warner that helped to make the Iron Works one of the city's most established foundries.

On the night of February 12, 1866, James Warner was crossing the street in front of the soldiers' barracks in Columbus, when an unknown assailant fired on him and shot him in the leg. Warner was immediately rushed to the local hospital where a team of surgeons amputated his wounded limb in an effort to save his life. The effort would be in vain. On the morning of February 22, 1866, Major Warner succumbed to his wounds, and the community mourned his loss tremendously. James Warner was laid to rest later that day at Linwood Cemetery.

Nearly 150 years have passed since Columbus's naval yard was lost to Wilson's raiders, but a strange and unusual phenomenon began to take place in the old Iron Works shortly after the death of James Warner. Because the Iron Works and the navy yard worked in unison during the manufacturing era, it seems typical that a ghost story or two would arise in regards to James Warner. It was rumored that after his death, a strange man in a blue overcoat wandered the upper floors, looking over the railings as if trying to keep watch over production. Though many reported seeing the man, upon investigation of the stranger, no one was ever able to find him, thus giving rise to the ghost of James Warner.

After the war, the Iron Works still mass-produced much of the same equipment as it did prior to the Civil War, including refrigerators and modern farm equipment. However, the unusual sightings of James Warner became less and less frequent as the years passed. In 1902, the foundry caught fire and burned a large part of the complex. Shortly after, reconstruction began for the second time, and the industry changed as steel was poured in the facility. Again, stories started to resurface regularly about a ghostly stranger in a blue coat that wandered the machine shop and other parts of the foundry.

In 1925, W.C. Bradley acquired the property and started manufacturing primarily for the hardware industry. Throughout the 1940s and 50s, more engineering evolved when the company began to manufacture parts for grills. In 1978, a small area of this once massive mill complex was set aside and would become today's Columbus Convention and Trade Center. The Columbus mills changed and evolved but generally stayed in a working order for more than 135 years, and it seems that the ghost of James Warner has also followed that change.

Even today, in its newly renovated state, the Columbus Convention Center is not without strange and unusual reports of the man in the blue coat. He is still seen hovering slightly among the rafters, as if walking on a ghostly platform and the same ghostly apparition has been seen on the lower floors of the building, disappearing through walls that lead to nowhere. Occasionally, employees and events staff have reported hearing unusual sounds coming from the building. The ghostly sounds of machinery seem to be a regular occurrence here, and the shouting of men who yell over their mechanical work environment is heard almost daily.

Today, the old foundries in Columbus have been silenced by age and modernization. The evolution of these companies may have been a critical part of business. Production on a mass scale takes time and a lot of skilled workers. But for James Warner and his crew of ghostly engineers, this job may never be done. The ghost of James Warner is still keeping watch over the industry he contributed so much to.

The Rankin House Spirit

Many fine homes dating back to the Victorian era can be found in Columbus's historical district. Most of these old homes have been completely renovated and are captivating to see up close. Cobblestone streets are still visible in some areas of the downtown and riverfront sections of Columbus, and large oaks cover the streets alongside budding crepe myrtles and massive magnolias. Glorious fountains spring water on humid days, and many tourists frequent the historical district to find out more about Columbus's past by visiting the large granite and marble monuments that mark historical accomplishments.

One home along Second Avenue sits apart from all the others—the Rankin House. It is located at 1440 Second Avenue in Columbus and was the home of James Rankin and his wife, Agnes, who emigrated from Scotland sometime before 1850. James was a planter, an established businessman and was also the owner of the Rankin Hotel, located downtown. Both the Rankin home and the hotel have a handful of ghost stories. The Rankin Hotel's notoriously haunted "Apartment M" has reportedly had occurrences of unusual thumping and scratching sounds for many years. Witness accounts from a Miss Georgia competitor and actors from the Springer Opera House all staying at the Rankin Hotel have come forward with these claims.

Construction on the Rankin House started prior to the Civil War and was overseen by a brickmason from South Carolina named Lawrence Wall, but the house was not completed until after the war ended. Prior to the Rankin family's occupation of the property, a camp was set up by Captain Garmany of a U.S. Marine Calvary Unit. The Marines camped here during the Indian Wars in 1836, and several men perished at the camp after fighting a heavily outnumbered battle in Girard. But despite the history of the property, the Rankins built their lavish home on the site, and James and Agnes lived in the home with their five children for many years.

The Rankins traveled frequently to Scotland and other parts of Europe to furnish their home with traditional European furniture and amenities. Most of these items can still be found at the Rankin House today. Several marble mantles, including the one in the dining room, are original to the home. In the north parlor, a curious mirror hangs and is also an original piece to the house. The cast-iron fence that surrounds the house once surrounded the home of General Henry Benning, located on Broadway Street. Gas lights were also part of the Rankin home and made it more modern than the majority of fine Columbus homes in that era. Also, the double staircase made of walnut was considered the grandest feature of the home because of its superior architecture. A newspaper article dated 1898 listed the Rankin Mansion as one of the finest homes in Columbus, and Mrs. Rankin had a particular flare for furnishing her home with the very best amenities.

Today, the Rankin House is home to the Historic Columbus Foundation and is open for tours, events, weddings and other recreation. Weddings are a big deal to any new bride and groom, and the lovely Rankin house is the perfect setting for a ceremony or reception, and the ghost of Mrs. Rankin seems to think so, too. It seems fitting that a woman with such grand taste and style would only continue with that same style in the afterlife. Many a bride married at the Rankin house can vouch for her strange and unusual way of making her presence known by aiding new brides with everything from wedding day jitters to lost items.

In 1992, a couple from Florida drove to Columbus to tour the house as a potential location for their wedding. They instantly fell in love with it and decided this would be where they would marry, since the groom was to be stationed at Fort Benning just after the wedding. On the wedding day, everyone gathered in the courtyard outside awaiting the ceremony. The bride was upstairs in one of the four bedrooms, which were used as a dressing area for bridesmaids and groomsmen. She was nervous and a bit rattled, as many first-time brides are, and she fumbled through boxes trying to find the rhinestone tiara for her veil. The tiara was a major part of her wedding day attire, and she panicked when she could not find the item.

The new bride wasn't feeling well, so she went into an upstairs bathroom. She wondered how she would make it through this day without something going terribly wrong. As she peered in the mirror, a female voice said, "Don't worry, lass; everything is going to be ok." Though it rattled her already frail nerves, she seemed to be strangely calmed by the voice. She left the bathroom and headed back to the dressing room. Her bridesmaids were in a panic, still looking for her tiara. The bride started to tear up a bit and said, "We are never going to find my tiara!" Just then, one of the bridesmaids came from the bathroom where the bride had just been and shouted, "I FOUND IT!" She rushed into the dressing room and handed the tiara to the bride.

The bride was mystified. Surely she didn't carry it into the bathroom where she was just moments before? She thought about the unusual voice she had heard and wondered if, in fact, she had heard the ghost of Agnes Rankin. Had Mrs. Rankin saved her wedding by assuring her it would be ok and helping her bridesmaids find the missing tiara?

Again, in 1994, a very young couple from Phenix City, Alabama married at the Rankin House. Many of their friends and family attended the ceremony, but a few came in late due to some heavy party activities the night before. One young lady attending the wedding with her best friend made her way upstairs to see Mindy, the bride, but seemed to have trouble finding the room she was in. She climbed the staircase to the upper floor and heard

The Rankin House is among many historical and haunted homes in Columbus, Georgia.

children giggling and laughing as she passed the door of the first bedroom. She opened the door to see if perhaps Mindy and her bridesmaids were in that room and discovered the room was empty.

She then moved toward the next door and heard running footsteps behind her. A gush of cold air blew past her and ruffled her dress. As she leaned over to straighten the dress, she glanced over to see who had run passed her in such a hurry and saw no one. She started to feel a little uneasy but knocked on the door and heard a voice say, "Come in." She pushed open the door, and there was Mindy and her bridesmaids. The young girl asked the other girls whose children were on the top floor making such a ruckus. When the bride said there were not any children there, the young lady became extremely nervous and went back down stairs. She told her friend, Noel, who attended the wedding with her, about what she had heard and felt upstairs. Noel just smiled at her and said, "You must still be hungover from last night."

In late 2000, a Columbus man approached the Rankin House about an event he wanted to hold for his business. He wanted the luncheon to be semiformal but in a fine-dining atmosphere. His colleagues gathered at the Rankin House on a Saturday evening and sat down for pleasant conversation and fine food. One of the catering staff was coming from the kitchen area to deliver food to the dining room and was holding a large tray of hors d'oeuvres. When he made his way to the threshold of the doorway, a woman in a long, dark dress appeared. Her hair was pulled up in a bun on the back of her head, and a large broach was pinned on her high collar. She stopped him and motioned for him to give her the tray.

Without saying a word he handed her the tray, and she made her way through the kitchen. He then noticed she was drifting effortlessly just above the floor. He turned back to his work, and a shiver ran up his spine when he realized that he may have just seen a ghost. He went back out into the house later and asked the event coordinator who had brought out the hors d'oeuvres. She shrugged her shoulders and gave a nod as if she was not certain. He later found out about the ghost of Agnes Rankin and assumed, as always, that Mrs. Rankin was keeping her guests happy and treating them to the very best.

Agnes Rankin isn't the only spirit at the Rankin House. People walking along the sidewalk outside the house at night have reported seeing shadows pass back and forth in the rear of the home. Though gated and locked occasionally, an oddly uniformed man is seen in the old stables out back. He is believed to be the spirit of a soldier named Thomas who died at the camp in 1836. His spirit roams the property freely and has been seen on the front lawn at the Rankin home. An old story handed down in one Columbus family tells of a cold, dark October evening, when some school children stopped at the corner of the Rankin yard and stood at the fence, daring each other to call out to the ghost of Thomas. They lined up at the fence and began to taunt the spirit but were quick to leave when a misty, white apparition appeared on the opposite side of the yard and slowly drifted across to them as it took the form of a uniformed Calvary scout.

Other, less frequent reports come from people who have seen Mrs. Rankin in the back courtyard wandering through the garden. She is always described as wearing the same dark dress with a high collar and antique broach, her dark hair always pulled up in a bun on the back of her head. She is never frightening, nor does she startle those who see her on purpose, but she does seem to insist on lending a hand even from the beyond. The laughing children, however, are still very much a mystery. Though a few other reports of the ghost of Thomas have surfaced over the years, none of them seem to be as prominent as Agnes Rankin.

She still keeps watch over her beautiful home and lends a ghostly hand to those who need it. She does not seem to mind sharing her mansion with the living, and perhaps she is still there because the children need looking after and maybe James as well. Her ghost seems to come and go as it pleases, perhaps, traveling the high seas to her home country of Scotland when sightings of her ghost are less frequent. She was determined in life to carry herself proudly in high society, and in death, it seems she continues to do the same. Should you find yourself in need of a beautiful, Victorian location for an event in Columbus, request a tour of the Rankin House, and should you decide to hold your event there, be sure to thank Mrs. Rankin for her generosity. She absolutely deserves it.

The Clock Ghost

In uptown Columbus, along Broadway Street, you can find several different curiosities and architectural wonders from the past. These include historical buildings, interesting landscapes and modern art provided by Columbus State University. Oddities that do not exist in most towns, like the *Man and Beast Fountain* designed to give water to the smallest and largest creatures, can also be found uptown. You can stop in the local pubs for a cold beverage and have a great meal at any of the modern dining restaurants or browse the shops for some great souvenirs. Spend an evening walking through the uptown district for a taste of local nightlife, listen to live musicians who play on weekend nights and take in all the sites and sounds of a wonderful and lively atmosphere.

The eclectic mixture of history and modern-day entertainment in Columbus may hide an intriguing feature of Broadway and perhaps a ghost or two. Many jewelry shops can be found on Broadway and have been located there for many years. Businesses on Broadway Street may come and go, but some business owners do not. In 1872, a German-born immigrant named Carl Frederick Schomburg came to Columbus and established himself as a watchmaker and jeweler. He was a pioneer in the early days of Columbus and had a somewhat formidable personality. He was an active member of the historical society, public library, local athletic and gun clubs, and he was also well known for his hard work and honesty in the community.

Schomburg died in 1937 and is buried in Section 6 of the Riverdale Cemetery, located on Victory Drive. His body has been laid to rest, but his spirit refuses to pass over. Rumor has it that he is still seen on Broadway Street late in the evening hours, when the streets are quiet and all the vendors and weekend events have gone. The apparition of an unusually dressed stranger, sometimes in a top hat and with a cane, has been seen near the old clock on Broadway in front of the jewelry store. Most of the reports from those who have seen this gentlemen note his striking resemblance to Carl Schomburg. Other reports associated with his ghost suggest that when he is seen near the old clock, those brave enough to approach the apparition can only get within arms reach of him before he disappears into a cloud of white smoke.

Others say that when you pass the old Broadway Street clock late at night, its hands spin uncontrollably and even backwards. Most assume it's nothing more than a faulty mechanical problem, but coupled with the ghostly apparition of the jeweler's ghost, even a faulty street clock can be a bit disturbing. No real evidence exists that the Broadway phantom is indeed Carl Schomburg, but the coincidence of the spirit in the clock is highly unusual. While walking home from your evening events on Broadway Street, do not forget to pass by the old clock and check the time. If your timing is right, the gentleman ghost of Broadway may make an appearance for you.

THE REMINISCENCE OF THE RIVERWALK

For hundreds of years, the Creek Indians called the banks of the Chattahoochee River their home, in what is today Phenix City, Alabama, and Columbus, Georgia. The Creeks lived in a location called Coweta Town. The Coweta Tallahassee people were also known as Lower Creeks and lived in relative harmony prior to their removal in 1830. The Cow Creeks (as they are sometimes referred to) of this area built large, earthen foundations, on which they built their living structures. Each tribe lived and worked in a community, and farming, fishing and gathering were the common tasks of everyday life.

The shoals brought neighboring tribes from both sides of the river together for fishing and recreation. Women and girls brought hand-woven baskets and fish traps to catch the shad, bass and sunfish that were abundant here. Young boys, skilled in bow fishing, accurately speared large catfish in the shallows, and some even lassoed huge lake sturgeon and brought them to shore. Children played in the cool baths of the Chattahoochee, which were a welcoming relief in the spring when daytime temperatures could get as high as eighty degrees.

The Yuchi tribes (also spelled Uchee) lived just across the river on the Georgia side of the Chattahoochee, and though this tribe was relatively different from the Cow Creeks, it lived much in the same way, depending on farming, fishing and gathering to provide for its people. The Yuchi people, however, had more of a tendency for war, and its settlement was known as the "Red" or "War Town."

For many years prior to the Indian Removal Act, voyagers from England, Spain and even France found their way to these native towns that dotted the River for hundreds of miles. The Spanish fought with the Yuchi and Creek tribes for allegiance, and in the early seventeenth century, the Spanish burned the Indian cities, forcing the Creek and Yuchi tribes to relocate. The Coweta Creek people moved to what is today Macon, Georgia, on the Ocmulgee River. Later, after the Yamasee War of 1715, the natives were forced to relocate once more but settled again on the Chattahoochee River.

Years of relocating and constant uprisings against white settlers over land and territories would make life very difficult for these people, and soon tribes would be split in half and forced to live in separate locations. The New or Upper Creek tribes were located upriver from their original location of Coweta Town. Those Creeks were descendants of the original Coweta people, and their culture was already mixed with the settlers in the area.

Benjamin Hawkins was an Indian agent from North Carolina, and he lived within the Creek territory. He had a Creek woman as his partner and had many children. Hawkins wanted to implement "civilized culture" within the native tribes and organize stability by giving them jobs as farmers, stockman and weavers. However, once the Indian Wars of 1812 progressed, the divided Creek tribes were becoming increasingly hostile toward one another. Though Benjamin Hawkins had always tried to keep peace among the Lower Creeks (or White Sticks as they were later known as), his efforts were not met with understanding by the Upper Creeks (also known as Red Sticks). The Red Sticks were becoming desperate to cling to their traditional native culture and beliefs.

Captain William McIntosh of Savannah was stationed in the Creek Territory during this time and took not one, but two Indian wives. In 1775, William McIntosh, the son of Captain William McIntosh was born. He held a prominent status in the Creek community and was raised by his mother, who was a Creek woman. The Creek people called him *Taskanugi Hatke*, which meant "White Warrior." William McIntosh, however, met an ill fate when he was executed by his own people in 1825 after he was accused of smuggling African slaves. He was also charged for collaborating with a U.S. Indian agent and helping draft the fraudulent Treaty of Indian Springs.

The Indian way of life was slowly dying, and new European ways were being forced onto the Creeks and Yuchis, causing them to be forced off their ancestral lands and dividing their people. Soon, uprisings of hostile tribes began to become an almost regular occurrence throughout many Indian territories.

A small band of Yuchi and Creek Indians from the settlements of Coweta and Yuchi, under the command of the infamous Chief Jim Henry, banded together to form an uprising, and on Friday, May 13, 1836, the band of hostile natives launched an attack on two steamships that were located on the Chattahoochee River. The hostile natives swiftly boarded the *Georgian*, and every person on board was murdered, except for an engineer who narrowly escaped. The ship was then burned. The *Hyperian* was anchored just two miles up the river and was attacked in much the same manner; however, the captain and two women did manage to escape, but the ship was set afloat, and it drifted until it hit a sandbar.

The outlaw group then crossed the river and descended on the unassuming town of Roanoke, Georgia, in Stewart County on the night of May 14, 1836. Reports from the small militia that was set up to defend the settlement state that strange hoots emanated from the surrounding forests that night. Most of the camp suggested that the sounds were nothing more than common sounds of nature. However, the small band of militia who were designated to protect the settlement had no idea that they were being surrounded by the same murderous group of Indians who had attacked the steamers the day before.

This tiny community was known as Little Hamlet, and most of the reports that stem from this particular episode suggest that the camp was relatively quiet that night and that the militia troop retired to its camp houses, as did the inhabitants of this small community. But early on the morning of May 15, 1836, the inhabitants of the quiet town who lay sleeping in their beds had no idea what terror surely awaited them. The war party of hostile Indians approached the settlement, and in a sudden strike, the natives let out blood-curdling war cries and rained down a hail of gunfire and assaults on every man, woman and child they could find.

Within a short length of time, the raiders had killed and scalped nearly every inhabitant of Little Hamlet, leaving very few survivors. Other reports suggest that only a few townspeople were killed, but official reports fail to mention the many who were injured and even missing, a cruel and brutal reminder of how dangerous frontier life was.

Shortly after this atrocity, most of the rouge tribe were apprehended and sent to different locations for imprisonment until trial. Six of these Creek and Yuchi Indians were captured near Columbus. They were tried and sentenced to death, and on the morning of November 26, 1836, those six Indians were hanged in an area located on the Alabama side of the Chattahoochee River, near what is today the Dillingham Street Bridge.

This part of the Riverwalk on the Phenix City side of the Chattahoochee River is said to be haunted by the six Indians who were hanged here.

Public execution was a morbid form of entertainment during this time in American history, and many townspeople from Alabama and Georgia flocked to witness the execution. All six of the Indians' names are perhaps lost to history, though. Four were discovered during research for this story: Co-in-chi-na, Tus-coo-ner, Clis-ar-ne-ha and Tim-a-sc-ha. These men died a very heroic death according to those who were witness to the event. A practice common among Indian warriors is the pride they show in the face of fear and death. Standing tall like the great bear, they welcome death as if it was a close but forgotten friend.

Today, the areas of the Creek and Yuchi settlements are covered by concrete sidewalks that range for several miles on both the Alabama and Georgia sides of the Chattahoochee River. The Riverwalk has long welcomed people who bike, hike and fish the areas, but also those who seek out a little piece of history. These areas can sometimes become flooded during periods of extreme rainfall, and Indian relics and artifacts are still found on occasion.

Most people, while enjoying a blissful stroll along the Riverwalk, are completely unaware they are being followed by the spirits of those forgotten Creek and Yuchi people. Many stories told over the years have come to describe the Indian spirits who haunt the Riverwalk, in particular the area where the six Indians were hanged to death. These river spirits are said to have scared the daylights out of those brave enough to go onto the Riverwalk at night. Strange sounds that seem like haunting remnants of Indian war cries hang in the air near this location, and creeping shadows are seen in the shrubbery along the wooded trails. One has to wonder if these are real people waiting to mug a passerby or if they are the ghosts of disgruntled natives. Either way, it would be wise to avoid the area after dark.

Even the more open areas of recreation have haunting tales of supernatural forces that linger in the area. Many report that these Indian spirits will follow bike riders, some on horseback, and others have been said to leap from trees overhead and into the bikers' path, causing many bike-related injuries as the apparitions are so real that people tend to think they are avoiding a living person. However, upon investigation of these "leapers," there is no one to be found.

Some of the other sightings tell of the Indian maiden who has been seen near the end of the Riverwalk near Golden Park. It's a common tale that this maiden is looking for a lost child who perhaps drowned in the river. She cries in desperation to find her lost little one. Many boaters in the area call her the "banshee," which is an Irish word that means "screaming ghost." She has also been seen at the sight of many boating accidents on the river, giving her a foul reputation.

Whatever the case may be, the Riverwalk definitely has some strange and unusual stories, some of which span back decades in time. Many more reports of these ghostly sightings have come out over the past few years, and it's possible that the newly dammed area of the Chattahoochee River has cut off some sort of supernatural life force to the location, again, forcing the native people to relocate to other areas of the river. This gives the term "uprising" a whole new meaning. If the destruction of the Creek territory was enough to unsettle these peaceful people from their homeland, what's to keep their spirits from doing the same?

The Phantom at Eubanks Field

Fort Benning's Airborne School, also known as "Jump School," involves a multitude of different aspects of training. While attending Airborne School at Fort Benning, a soldier can expect three weeks of hard-core training that involves strenuous exercise, learning the fine points of a parachute, parachute landing fall techniques (PLF), jump training and jumping from a B18 aircraft.

The first week of training consists of a lot of physical training (PT). Being physically fit is an important part of any military training exercise. Jumping from several hundred feet in the air with a fifty pound parachute strapped to your back is dangerous enough without the proper instruction, so classes given by military instructors called "black hats" are critical in learning how a parachute functions and what to expect when exiting an aircraft, as well as the proper procedures to keep soldiers safe.

Week two of jump school consists of training in mock fashion. This is usually the time when students are introduced to Eubanks Field at Fort Benning. The location is designed to train soldiers by using mock setups that simulate aircraft-related aspects of training. It also gives the student the ability to understand how parachute rigging works and what to do in the event of an emergency if a parachute malfunctions or if it is not deployable. The jump towers at Eubanks Field also were once used to help paratroopers understand what it was like to descend under a canopy.

In May 1941, two of the jump towers located on Eubanks field at Fort Benning were completed. In November that year, the third tower was completed, and the fourth was finished a month later. In the early 1960s, the towers were a common part of training and were frequently used during the second and third weeks of training. Large buildings located under the towers housed four elevator motors that powered the contraption by raising the jumper more then two hundred feet in the air. Eight cables were attached to the rigging devices that held the canopy, and jumpers were strapped securely inside special harnesses to keep them safe. Once raised to the top of the tower, the jumpers were released, and the parachute would descend to the ground.

The jump towers were used for several years without incident; however, more and more accidents started to become a common thread when using the towers and the towers were eventually closed down. In March 1954, one of the four towers at Eubanks Field was destroyed when a tornado touched down. This should have been a heavenly omen to bring them all down, but the towers were opened again and used for training once more.

Though reports are scarce, a few deaths are rumored to have taken place due to accidents involving the jump towers. A retired jumpmaster described an accident he witnessed in the mid-1960s. While watching his students descend from the tower, a harness in the rigging snapped and failed to deploy the canopy properly. The soldier fell more than sixty feet to the ground, and his injuries were extensive. The accident resulted in several broken bones in his face, ribs, leg and both arms. Though he survived the fall, his body would eventually succumb to the trauma, paralyzing him. The soldier lived only a few weeks and died of complications from pneumonia. Shortly after, students and black hats alike started to notice unusual things happening around the towers.

Lights inside the elevator houses would come on when no one was inside. One instructor who witnessed this said he went inside to see if some of his jump school trainees were perhaps planning a prank of some sort. When he entered the building, he searched the entire location and found no one. Shortly after the first report, students would notice rigging and harnesses would go missing before exercises. More accidents began to take place, and once again, the towers were closed due to the great potential for someone else to get hurt or worse.

Today, thousands of students come to Jump School at Fort Benning every year. Eubanks field is still a working facility (except for the jump towers), and there are still unusual reports of ghostly phenomenon associated with the location. The story of the Phantom at Eubanks Field is a common one, and his supernatural shenanigans have some soldiers shaking in their boots.

The jump towers located at Eubanks Field on Fort Benning are rumored to be haunted by the spirit of a jump school student who fell to his death in the 1960s.

From surrounding neighborhoods, located across the street from Eubanks Field, to the airborne barracks located several hundred feet away, there have been weird sightings of an unusual soldier in an out-dated uniform walking with a strange kink in his step.

Of course, many speculate that he is merely the harmless ghost of the airborne soldier killed in the rigging accident. Others will beg to differ to the harmless nature of this spirit. On one such occasion, a fire drill was conducted at 04:00 a.m., and all soldiers evacuated the barracks. The sergeants in charge of the fire drill exercises then cleared the barracks by checking to see that all the soldiers had safely exited the building. In doing so, a sergeant walked into one of the facilities and saw a young man lying facedown on the floor at the end of the hallway. He approached the man, kneeling down to turn him over, and saw that his face had been crushed. Blood and bone fragments were shattered all about the floor, and upon further investigation, he noticed that the man's body was positioned awkwardly. The sergeant panicked and ran to get help. When he returned, he could not find the wounded soldier or any sign that he was there.

He thought surely the wounded soldier must have woken up and walked away, but no man with injuries that extensive could have just walked away! And not a single drop of blood could be found in the area where he had been. Another situation was reported within the last ten years of a similar apparition seen by families living in the housing area near Eubanks Field. One mother called the military police when her four-year-old son came running to her in fear. He screamed and cried that an "army man" with a bloody face was looking at him through his bedroom window. The only problem was that his bedroom window was on the top floor of a two-story housing unit. This would have meant that the face that he saw was more then twenty feet off the ground.

Other reports from Eubanks Field have been in circulation for several generations now. Everything from flashing lights near the towers at night to shadowy figures that walk through the open areas and vanish into thin air have been reported, but the strange circumstances surrounding the soldier killed in the rigging accident always seem to spark up a tale or two on a regular basis. No one knows the identity of the man or has any idea why on earth his spirit chose to stay in an endless course of airborne training. Perhaps it's more of a notion of leaving something incomplete. Soldiers are taught from their first day of training to never give up on themselves and complete the task at hand. Maybe this is what the phantom of Eubanks Field is doing, still trying to meet his goals that he fell short of so long ago.

The Old Station Hospital

The old Camp Benning infirmary once stood near Baltzell Avenue located on Fort Benning. After several years, it was replaced by the station hospital that was completed in 1925. It was used as a working medical facility until 1958. When Martin Army Community Hospital opened, the old station hospital was used as a clinic and an extension of the new hospital. When it was closed again in 1975, renovations were under way to reconstruct the building as the National Infantry Museum. The museum opened in 1977 and housed a variety of historical artifacts and information until 2008. In 2009, the new infantry museum was opened at 1775 Legacy Way in Columbus, and the old station hospital once again sat empty.

The old station hospital has long been a source of rumor and legend associated with ghosts and spirits. Some say the old artifacts from the museum left a strange impression on the building, causing restless spirits to attach themselves to their personal property and linger about the old building, looking for the objects that once belonged to them. Others say the ghostly inhabitants are the poor souls that died from injury or illness while at the old station hospital.

Today the old station hospital, once again is undergoing another reconstruction. The old hospital has been gutted and looks to be nothing more then a lifeless old dilapidated structure. But contractors and visitors to the facility say the building is still very much alive. During World War II, the old station hospital was a busy hub for injured and ill soldiers returning from war. Many men returning from the battlefields of Europe found comfort in the facility, but others did not. Some soldiers returned from war in terrible condition due to illness and or injury, and nearly 3,600 men were treated in the old station hospital during World War II, and some of these spirits still roam this skeletal structure that make up the building compound.

A story has long circulated about two brothers divided by war, but brought together again at the old station hospital after they were both injured in separate battles in Germany. Both men were said to have been brought to the old station hospital just weeks apart. When Private Murphy arrived at Fort Benning and was admitted to the hospital for gangrene, he learned that his brother was also en route to Fort Benning and was to be admitted to the hospital as well. Before the Murphy boys could be reunited, the eldest died from his infection. Not long after his brother finally arrived and learned of his brother's passing, he, too, passed away within days of his arrival.

The brothers are rumored to have finally been reunited in death and have reportedly been seen in the hospital dressed in their traditional World War II military uniforms. Some stories of the brothers' ghosts tell of sightings of the men playing cards together, and the shuffling sound of cards is often heard near the old recreational area of the hospital, which is located on the bottom floor. Others have seen the misty apparitions of the brothers walking through the hallways in casual conversation.

Shortly after the old station hospital was converted to the Infantry Museum, rumors started circulating about the ghost of a confederate soldier who had been seen frequenting the housed artifacts (which is off limits to the public). One woman suggested that he may have been a casualty of war, but before the field hospital infirmary was built, there was no Civil War–related structure in the area and no battle-related history to identify the confederate spirit. However, other personnel who witnessed the haunt say this particular rumor may, in fact, be accurate. When the new location for the National Infantry Museum opened in 2009, and items and artifacts were moved from the old station hospital, the sightings of the confederate phantom stopped altogether. Did he perhaps follow his lost artifacts to the new location?

Other reports of paranormal activity at the old hospital include the spirit of a young woman who also haunts the hallways inside the building. This young female spirit is nearly always reported as having medium-length, reddish-blonde hair and wearing a standard hospital gown. She appears barefoot and in a rather sickly state, her pale skin riddled with sores that appear to be open and bleeding. It's possible she could have been a victim of a measles epidemic or another disease that was widespread in the early nineteenth century.

The old Station Hospital located on Fort Benning, built in 1925, is undergoing another transformation.

She has been known to glide among the upper floor hallways and in and out of rooms. Another common location for her spirit is the outside balconies where she would appear and disappear. Since the new renovation of the building many people have come forth with unusual stories about all kinds of paranormal phenomenon that has taken place here. Just recently, four construction workers working on the building stated that moaning sounds could be heard in the east wing of the building in the evenings, when everyone is getting ready to go home. For several days, the men heard the sounds and ignored it. After an afternoon of working in the east wing, the men looked diligently for the source of the strange moaning sound and turned up nothing. There is no power in the building, and most of the electricity provided to the workers was produced by generators.

Others have reported similar sounds but coupled with frantic screams and wails like that of a woman being tortured. Another story came about in the late 1940s of a female nurse who was said to have fallen in love with a major who was a doctor at the facility. After many months of working together, she approached him with her feelings, only to be turned down by the major. It's rumored she flung herself from the upper balcony of the nurses barracks and died a painful and heartbreaking death. These female screams are said to be her cries of heartache.

While most of the legends and stories associated with the old station hospital are purely myth, one cannot dismiss the claims of so many. Could it simply be power of suggestion stirring up the phantoms or overactive imaginations? Could there really be some spirits bound to the old station hospital? Hospitals will always be associated with healing and unfortunate suffering, a house that holds the sick and the dying. And even after eighty years, the old station hospital is still holding onto hers.

UNSOLVED MYSTERIES

THE STOCKING STRANGLER MURDERS

Discussing haunted locations in and around the city of Columbus can be a controversial subject for residents. One such subject of controversy revolves around one of Columbus's own unsolved mystery and the paranormal activity associated with the locations impacted by the "Stocking Strangler" murders.

Many people all over the world are familiar with the story of the Big Eddy Club killings and the story behind the man allegedly responsible for the rape and murders of several prominent women in the Wynnton area of Columbus. Carlton Gary was indicted and charged for three of the seven murders that took place over an eight-month period between 1977 and 1978. Dubbed the "Stocking Strangler" by the media, he was reported to have killed his victims by strangulation with a pair of panty hose after he had beaten and raped them.

Other unusual circumstances involving the case of the Stocking Strangler have come to light since 2009. Gary's case was reevaluated after DNA evidence turned up that linked him to other crimes in New York, but the evidence was inconclusive in regards to the crimes that took place in Columbus. This suggested Gary may have been innocent of some of the crimes he was charged with in Columbus and that the real killer could possibly still be at large.

Today, several of the Stocking Strangler murders are still open and unsolved. Several aspects of this case have thrown a monkey wrench in conclusively identifying Gary as the actual killer involved. Though evidence that ties him into some aspects of the crimes exists, he has avoided Georgia's death penalty thus far and, in 2009, was granted a stay of execution by the State of Georgia under the grounds of "reasonable doubt," meaning there is simply not enough proof to establish him as the actual killer.

With the burden of proof weighing heavily on Gary, his alleged victims are burdened as well. Some speculate that the spirits of these murdered women seek a vengeful justice. Several of the locations associated with the crime scenes are reported to be ripe with paranormal activity. The first victim of the Stocking Strangler was a public health official named Ferne Jackson. She was a widowed, fifty-nine-year-old woman with no children of her own. She was dropped off the night before she was murdered, in September 1977, by a friend who attended a bible study class with Ferne at the St. Luke's United Methodist Church on Second Avenue.

She was found the following morning by authorities when she did not report for work. She had been strangled to death in the bedroom of her home on Seventeenth Street. Part of the house had been ransacked, and the murder weapon, hosiery tied to a dressing-gown cord, lay just next to her body. Her spirit is said to still inhabitant her former home, roaming the hallways at night in a satin nightgown in search of her killer.

The second victim was Florence Scheible. She was eighty-nine years old and lived on Dimon Street, just a few blocks from the initial crime scene of Ferne Jackson. She was also found strangled to death in her home on October 21, 1977. Her ghost is reported to still frequent her former neighborhood. Some residents of Dimon Street report seeing the apparition of an elderly lady, also dressed in a nightgown, who wanders up and down the neighborhood sidewalks. Though Florence Scheible was, in fact, the Stocking Strangler's second victim, a local criminal came forth a few days before this event and admitted that he was responsible for raping and murdering the two elderly women. The only problem with his confession was that he was in police custody when the murder of Florence Scheible occurred.

Not long after, a third victim was found. Jean Dimenstein was found murdered in much the same fashion as Florence Scheible, and at this point, the City of Columbus was in a great state of panic. The Columbus Police Department had upgraded patrols in the Wynnton area and called on military volunteers from Fort Benning to help aid in the manhunt of the brutal serial killer.

The home of the fourth victim of the Stocking Strangler, Kathleen Woodruff, once stood at 1811 Buena Vista Road and has since been torn down, but her spirit is still reported to roam the area. The elderly woman's ghost is rumored to appear on moonlit nights in the area where the home stood. Many people who have visited this location while following the trial suggest that her spirit is willingly reaching out to anyone who will listen. This ghostly apparition has been seen wearing a red scarf, which was reported to have been found wrapped around her neck at the crime scene.

On February 11, 1978, Mrs. Ruth Schwob was the fifth victim in the series of attacks; however she survived the brutal assault due to the crafty nature of her neighbor who had wired his own alarm system into her house. When she was found several minutes after her home alarm alerted neighbors and authorities, she had just regained consciousness after nearly being choked to death by the strangler. Police made a diligent effort to locate the suspect after the attack, but they were not successful. Unfortunately, on that very night, the Stocking Strangler murdered again in the midst of the search to find him. Mildred Borom lived in at 1612 Forest Avenue just two blocks away from Ruth Schwob. Sadly she, too, was found murdered in the same manner as all the previous victims.

Because the strain of the killings had begun to take a toll on the community and the Columbus Police Department, authorities turned to a controversial method of investigation. A well-known psychic named John Argeris was notified of the slayings in Columbus, and he agreed to

Part of the Wynnton area of Columbus where the Stocking Strangler Murders took place.

help police in the search for potential information regarding the identity of the Stocking Strangler. Argeris received messages through clairvoyance and communication with the dead victims that led him to believe that the identity of the Stocking Strangler was that of a white male who was from the area and that this man had rather large eyes and a full beard and most likely went by John.

In just a few months, the last and final victim of the Stocking Strangler, Janet Cofer was killed on April 20, 1978. She was a sixty-one-year-old elementary schoolteacher who resided on Steam Mill Road, a few miles from the Wynnton area. For eight months, authorities struggled to catch the serial killer who had terrorized Columbus, and as abruptly as the murders began in September 1977, they stopped with the murder of Janet Cofer in April 1978.

Today, the circumstances involving these murders are still a great mystery. Most folks agree that the evidence presented against the suspect involved is merely superficial and that there is indeed a killer who got away with murder, but the ghosts of these murdered women still are earthbound, destined to see the day that their killer is brought to justice. Many believe that he is still out there; others believe he may have passed on into the spirit realm himself. Either way, his fate is sealed, for the spirits that long for justice in this matter will not rest until he is punished for his crimes or joins them in the realm of the dead.

THE DILLINGHAM STREET BRIDGE

In 1830, construction plans for the lower city bridge known as the Dillingham Street Bridge were laid out, and master engineer John Godwin and his slave and master bridge builder, Horace King, were contracted to build one of the city's first bridges. The bridge would connect Columbus to Girard, Alabama, what is today Phenix City.

Horace King was born into slavery in South Carolina. His family had a diverse background of African American, Catawba Indian and European ancestry. John Godwin purchased the King family at a slave auction in South Carolina and moved to Girard, Alabama. Godwin realized the genius in King early on and treated him essentially as a business partner rather than a slave. John Godwin and Horace King gained many favorable contracts in bridge building, and bridges built by the pair can be found from Alabama to South Carolina.

When the plans for Columbus's lower city bridge were finished, Godwin and King set right to work, erecting a covered bridge that spanned 560 feet across the Chattahoochee River, connecting Girard and Columbus. In the spring of 1865, Union forces were fast approaching the Girard area in an effort to gain control over Columbus and its armory and navy yard. On April 4, 1865, the Confederate army had all but dwindled away and few Confederate forces remained in Girard and Columbus. In the early evening hours, a small Confederate unit, under the command of Captain Nat Clanton, fell under attack near Summerville Road in Girard and was quickly over taken by the Union forces lead by General James Wilson.

The Dillingham Street Bridge was the site of a violent and fiery Civil War skirmish.

Wilson's raiders headed for the Dillingham Street Bridge, and under the cover of darkness, the Union calvary approached the bridge. As they got closer they realized that this small unit of Confederate soldiers had anticipated their attack and the rebel soldiers had pulled up the floor boards of the bridge on the approaching side. They also placed large bails of cotton soaked in turpentine under the remaining floor joist.

As the Union forces dismounted and headed for the bridge, an onslaught of Union infantryman made considerable headway across the disabled structure. As the Confederates watched the Union soldiers approach their position, the small unit disbursed, and an unorganized, chaotic chain of events started to unfold.

The Confederates scrambled as they set for the bridge with horses, buggies and everything they could carry, fearing they had been cut off. The Union army scrambled as well, and men and animals clashed in the darkness. Without even a sliver of moonlight, both armies were locked tight on the failing bridge, embraced in battle against an opponent they could not see. Muskets fired and sabers sparked in the dark. Brothers and countrymen alike were struck by their own forces, and men fell from the bridge into the river below. Horses and buggies shifted the weight on the unsteady bridge and the Union forces pushed the Confederates back onto the Georgia side.

Just as the Confederates had all but given up hope, a brave and noble Confederate soldier made one last desperate attempt to hold the bridge. Colonel C.C. McGhee grabbed a faintly lit torch that had all but smoldered out and crawled onto the dilapidated bridge. He prayed that God would make him swift, for this was the last hope to save Columbus from the impending Union force. Colonel McGhee struggled on his hands and knees until he found a small section of wooden planks that had been saturated with turpentine. He blew vigorously on the embers of the torch. Suddenly, a small spark arose from the torch, and Colonel McGhee quickly laid the small flame down on the oily wood.

Violent flames erupted from the ignition of oil, and the flames quickly spread across the entire length of the bridge. Suddenly, the site of blue and grey uniforms were visible, and the bodies of those lost in battle lay riddled across every inch of the old bridge, a grizzly site that would strike the strongest soldier to his knees. Even though both armies fought diligently to hold the bridge, the Union forces were eventually victorious. The Confederate stronghold was easily overcome due to lack of man power. This would be the last battle of the Civil War, the battle of Girard.

The Dillingham Street Bridge was later rebuilt, again by Horace King and John Godwin, and it was built one more time, being redesigned and constructed with concrete. Today, the bridge is a quiet reminder of the Battle of Girard, but the Civil War soldier who haunts the bridge is not so quiet. Most of the Riverwalk recreation area is connected to the Dillingham Street Bridge, but locals who are familiar with the area stay clear of the bridge, especially at night. A Confederate soldier is still seen on the bridge wandering back and forth, seemingly lost in time and lost in the chaos and pitch black of the Battle of Girard that more than likely took his life.

Rumor has it that this undead soldier paces the length of the bridge back and forth with a black powder rifle flung over his shoulder, dressed in his grey Confederate uniform and wearing a short brim infantry cap. He guards the bridge some 147 years after the battle of Girard, waiting for the next attack and ready to defend the bridge at all cost.

The Supernatural Stage Coach Inn

Just a few miles outside of Columbus is the sleepy little town of Waverly Hall. Waverly Hall has been virtually unchanged outside of a few modern amenities since its infancy. Many old plantation homes can be found in the community that bring back the southern charm and rich history of the pre–Civil War era. One such home is the old Stage Coach Inn. The home is the residence of the Adams family today. The Adams have painstakingly poured their devotion and love of the old home into every nail and floorboard to bring it back to its original state but have also discovered that more than a few ghosts still reside in their historical home.

The Stage Coach Inn was originally built in 1824 to house travelers on the stagecoach overnight. At that time, it consisted of two log cabins that had interior doors facing the opposite building. The logs were held together with red clay, a very prominent material in Georgia, and coaches could pull in between the cabins and unload passengers and luggage. Men and women were separated into the different cabins and wooden cots or perhaps bunks were used for beds.

Early historical records show letters written in journals from female travelers who stayed at the inn. The letters stated that it was sometimes a scary place to spend the night since the territory was still inhabited by Indians. The letters also reported seeing the Indians watching them through the logs where mortar was scarce. This must have been extremely unnerving for the women staying here because frequently women would be kidnapped or carried off by hostile Indians in these primitive territories. Traveling by stagecoach in this part of the South was a dangerous and treacherous journey in the early 1800s, but it was also the only means of transportation until the railroad system was introduced to southwest Georgia in 1830.

Eventually the old Stage Coach Inn was used as a dormitory in the early1830s. Workers who helped build and rebuild railways, other men who helped in contracted work and possibly even soldiers who fought during the American Indian Wars were housed in the dormitory. In the late 1830s, the inn was turned into a home owned by Major Thomas Camp and his family. The two log cabin structures were joined in the middle with a hallway and staircase, and a large porch wrapped the distance of the front of the home and part of the sides. The Camp family lived at the Stage Coach for many years and was a very prominent family in Waverly Hall. Many graves with the surname Camp can still be found today in the family plot in the Waverly Hall Cemetery.

Major Thomas Camp had a lovely daughter named Octavia. She married Doctor Benjamin Nathan Bussey in 1888 and lived in the Camp home where Doctor Bussey's office was located. Horses and carriages were parked on the outside near a dirt service road, and benches lined the small porch outside his office. Doctor Bussey was a well respected physician in the area and was loved by everyone in the community.

The Stage Coach Inn, located in Waverly Hall, was once a double log cabin used to house travelers overnight on the stagecoach routes.

Today, the Adams family has made some tremendous discoveries in the old stagecoach home that helps tell the story and solidifies much of its history and of its haunting as well. Recently, several medical books were found in the barn on the property by the youngest daughter, Jasmin. She has also encountered several phantoms in the home. She frequently hears footsteps on the upper floor that seem to travel from room to room and the sound of a bouncing ball. On one occasion, she heard something move in her bedroom and upon investigation found that a clock, conveniently fashioned into an ornamental stagecoach, had been moved from the fireplace mantle onto her bedroom dresser. She has also seen an apparition who she believes to be Doctor Bussey. While in the area of the home that was used as the doctor's office, she stumbled onto a chilling sight when she passed an open doorway. First, she heard voices, and when she turned to acknowledge the conversation, she saw a man dressed strangely in what she described as old-fashioned attire. He appeared to be talking to a female patient who likely had a knee injury of some sort. When Jasmin made eye contact with the two ghostly beings, she immediately turned to run. When she looked back, they had disappeared.

According to P.J. Adams, none of the spirits at the Stage Coach Inn seem to be violent or malicious, but those types of circumstances involving physically seeing full-bodied apparitions do tend to be a bit frightening. "It's just really weird," Jasmin said. Efforts continue to restore the home to its original state, and Mrs. Adams believes the spirits of the Stage Coach are quite comfortable knowing their celestial home is staying in its original state and believes the spirits are most comfortable in knowing that.

This may be the case since other reports tell of a man who has been seen in a military uniform walking down a stairway that has long been removed and boarded up. Inside a downstairs closet, the Adams discovered half a staircase that once led to the upper floor prior to the middle section of the house being added. This staircase was uncovered, and several small objects had been found that were left on the steps, including a candy dish and a man's wallet made of lambskin. Prior to the Adams' purchase of the home, a former owner did find the doctor bag owned by Doctor Bussey in the house but later sold it.

A few rumored deaths are also closely associated with the home. Rumor has it that a legend evolved over the years of a Yankee soldier who was thrown in the well outside the old inn. Although it's possible he was an intruder on the property during the Civil War and was killed and thrown into the well, it isn't likely, since the well was the only water source at the time. However, it is likely that the soldier could have simply drowned in the well under accidental circumstances.

The supernatural atmosphere at the Stage Coach Inn isn't a daily occurrence, but unusual activity does take place on a fairly regular basis. Recently, a psychic medium attended an investigation at the Stage Coach Inn and relayed a lot of information to the Adams family regarding the spirits at the home. While one precognitive suggestion went undetermined for the better part of a year or more, it came to light recently, shortly after the interview for this story. A local psychic, who wished to remain anonymous, told Mrs. Adams of a large wolf-like animal that she encountered in the kitchen. It was likely that this animal was of the spirit realm, and Mrs. Adams was perplexed at the notion of what this animal could be reference too.

However, the most recent report of the supernatural activity surrounding the old Stage Coach Inn came on May 4, 2012, when Mr. Adams encountered a huge wolf–like animal in his front yard, under the light of this year's largest full moon. The beast attacked one of the family pets, a small rabbit that was kept on the front porch. When Mr. Adams walked onto his porch, he was met at almost eye level with the creature. He waved his arms at it frantically, and it ran to the front yard, only a few feet away. There, it stood looking at Mr. Adams. Mr. Adams recalled thinking that the creature did not seem real; it was excessively large and had a strange demeanor.

Undeterred, Mr. Adams rescued the bunny and brought in inside, but the circumstances of the wolf-like creature has still left the family baffled. Is this the animal spirit the psychic told them about? Or could it be something else?

The Legacy of a Lycan

Supernatural tales of unusual beasts have long been a part of traditional Native American and European folklore. Most are dismissed today as simple myth or legend. But there is one tale of an unusual young girl, with perhaps an even more unusual condition, that can still be heard today in Talbot County, Georgia.

Talbot County was established in 1827 from land that was once part of Muscogee County. Some prominent European settlers had established themselves in fine antebellum homes and plantations in an area known as Woodland. One sophisticated and rather prominent family settled on Pleasant Hill near the Woodland area. Joel Burt and his wife, Mildred, had lived on their family plantation for many years and raised several children, until Joel's death at the age of forty.

Mildred still managed to take care of her large plantation and raise her children with help from her family who lived near by. Mildred had inherited a fine home, complete with a library and more than fifteen house slaves and field hands, numerous farm animals, a carriage and several hundred acres of land. After her husband's death, Mildred carried on the task of caring for their four children. Though most of the children were normal and had no unusual tendencies outside of childish antics, the middle child, Isabella, developed some strange behavioral problems in her late teen years.

Isabella was said to have an unusual appearance. She had an over-pronounced jaw, which caused a tremendous amount of dental problems for her, and her teeth were broken and sharp, so she rarely smiled. Her hair was dark brown, and her eyebrows were very thick. She was very withdrawn and had no desire for social contact outside of her immediate family. Isabella spent countless hours doing the one thing she loved—reading.

In the Burt home, an elaborate and well-furnished library was Isabella's domain. Mildred Burt, Isabella's mother, frequently traveled to many parts of Europe, including France, where she had relatives. Mildred brought back hundreds of books for Isabella, who had a passion for supernatural and paranormal literature. Isabella spent hours reading the strange tales of European superstitions, mythical creatures and legends of ghosts and goblins.

Sarah Burt, Isabella's older sister was not as withdrawn as her sibling and was, in fact, very sociable and well liked among the community. She struck a particular interest in a young man named William Gorman, who was a neighbor and son of a fellow plantation owner. He frequented the Burt home often while courting Miss Sarah Burt, and the two planned to marry.

One evening, William came to the Burt home and informed his fiancé Sarah that there had been some strange mutilations of his sheep and that other farmers in the area had started to report the same. The animals were slaughtered and ripped into shreds, but no meat was taken from the carcasses, and all the blood had been drained from the slain animals. Sarah curled her lip at the grotesque and vile report, but young Isabella took a peculiar interest in the subject. Isabella listened quietly from inside the window as William disclosed more of the gory details to Sarah. After William left, Isabella approached Sarah and demanded she tell her more about the mutilated sheep. Sarah was repulsed at the idea of retelling the horrible story and refused. Isabella became angry and grabbed Sarah by the arm, nearly tearing it off and dislocating it at the shoulder.

Isabella continued to have unusual episodes of mood swings, insomnia, violence and severe headaches. Mildred took Isabella to the local physician, and she was treated with opium to help dull the pain of her headaches. Mildred was becoming increasingly concerned for her daughter and began to monitor her day and night. Mildred kept Isabella in the library as much as possible in an effort to steer her clear of anyone witnessing her weird behavior or be a victim of her violent mood swings.

One night, with the moon set high in the sky, Mildred awoke to the rambling sounds of something moving inside the house. She opened her nightstand drawer and pulled from it a small caliber pistol, which she had also inherited from her late husband. Mildred was an expert markswoman and practiced shooting the antique pistols regularly. She feared an intruder might be in the house, so she slipped into her night coat, dimmed her lantern and set out into the dark house with her pistol drawn. She searched the house and did not find anyone. Nothing was out of place. Then, an unusual figure outside the window caught her attention. Mildred walked onto the porch and was shocked to see Isabella walking down the dirt path.

Mildred lowered her lantern and kept a fair distance from Isabella as she followed her daughter into the darkness. Isabella seemed frenzied and wild. She would bare her teeth like a rabid dog and scratched at the ground as she made her way toward a neighboring farmhouse. She stopped for a second and turned in the direction of her mother. Mildred quickly hid behind a large oak and doused the lantern under her finger tips. As she held her breathe, she peeked from behind the tree and saw Isabella sniffing the night air in an animal like trance. Isabella suddenly turned and tore through an open field toward a herd of cattle. As she approached the field, her mother watched from her hiding place. The moonlight served as her lantern as she watched Isabella violently chase the cattle and scratch and bite at them. Mildred was horrified at the sight but was helpless in the effort to collect her mentally unstable daughter. She slowly eased back into the shrubbery and made her way back to the house. Crying in desperation, she had no choice but to ignore the unusual behavior and hope that no one had witnessed Isabella's attack.

The following day, William Gorman returned to the Burt plantation and told Sarah and Mildred that animals had once again been slain in the night and that he was forming a posse of men to find and destroy the beast responsible for the carnage. Mildred knew what she had witnessed the night before and secretly hoped that some how she could hide Isabella's actions from William and the posse. Mildred asked William if she could join the posse and William accepted. Even though having a woman involved in a hunting party was unusual, he agreed since Mildred had expert marksmanship, and she would no doubt make a great asset in potentially killing the beast.

As it grew late, the sky filled with a dense purple and a blue haze that seemed to offset the light from the stars. The full moon rose quietly in the sky, and an odd orange glow began to fill the darkness like some strange aura. As the moon grew higher, the land was cast in the orange glow. Something strange was no doubt in order for this night.

The posse gathered at the Gorman plantation and with rifles, pistols and torches in hand. The men and Mrs. Burt set forth in the night to find the terrible beast. Hours past, and nothing could be found. The livestock were not alarmed, which was unusual for a full moon night. Mrs. Burt grew tired and retired herself from the group. William Gorman offered to walk her home, but Mrs. Burt insisted she travel home alone. After all, she was armed and was more than capable of taking care of herself. As Mildred traveled down the dirt path back to her home, she noticed movement in the bushes near the path she was on. She stopped and drew her pistol. A few seconds of silence passed, and suddenly, out of the dark, a figure lunged at her. It was the beast! Mildred fired a single shot, and the animal let out a deafening scream and ran back into the darkness.

Mildred thought to go back to the Gorman place but elected to make her way home as fast as she could to check on her own family. As Mildred approached her home, she saw a small, cowering, figure on her porch. As she approached the strange figure, she saw that it was Isabella. She was in a horrid and terrified state. Her face was pale, her hair was dirty and matted and she was sweating profusely. Mildred leaned down to aid her daughter, and as she lifted Isabella's body, she saw that her hand was mangled and virtually blown off. Mildred was horrified as she remembered the previous events that had taken place just a few minutes before. Mildred had shot at a beast but mangled her daughter at the same time.

Mildred rushed Isabella to the local doctor who tended to her wounded hand, and Mildred confided in him all the terrible circumstances that had happened over the last few weeks. The doctor suggested to Mildred that Isabella be sent away and studied. He told her about an unusual psychiatric condition called Lycanthropy. Lycanthropy is a mental condition that causes human beings to take on wolf-like characteristics. Generally, the condition is coupled with clinical depression, schizophrenia and bipolar disorders. Though many mental diseases were not studied in America at this time, doctors in parts of Europe during the period were treating mental patients for all sorts of defects and conditions.

Mildred had shot at a beast but mangled her daughter at the same time. *Illustration by Matthew Wertjes.*

Mildred agreed to have Isabella sent to Europe and arranged for her departure that night. As soon as Isabella was well enough to travel, Mildred sent her away and told her family and neighbors that Isabella was visiting relatives in France. Isabella was gone for many months, and the Woodland area had grown quiet. No reports of mutilations or massacred livestock had taken place.

Mildred soon received word from the physician in France who had been treating Isabella that she had been cured of her unusual condition and was fit to come home. Mildred was excited about the return of her daughter but told no one of her homecoming. The events of the shooting had been a rumor in Woodland for many months, and Mildred feared Isabella's mangled hand would surely give her unnatural state away and indicate the rumored events to be true.

Isabella arrived home and kept to herself. Again she took to the one thing she loved most, her books. Spending time in the library was her most beloved past time. Shortly after Isabella's return, rumors of more mutilations began to arise in the community, and Mildred kept an even closer eye on her. Though most of the reports were scarce, it raised a concern with Mildred. She knew what Isabella was capable of, for she had seen it with her own eyes.

Eventually, the reports of the slaughtered animals died out altogether, and Isabella Burt lived out her days in the Burt home until her death at age seventy in 1911. She was buried in the family cemetery located in Woodland. Isabella died having never been married and without children. This story has been shared on many occasions, and most folks have to agree to disagree on whether the legend of Isabella is truly based on fact or fiction. However, most folks in Talbotton, Georgia agree that even in this day and time, when the full moon rises high and casts an eerie red-orange glow, that the howls of wolves can be heard for miles, especially near the old Burt/Owen family cemetery where Isabella is buried. They seem to sing a ghostly chorus, as if in mourning for one of there own.

Occasionally, wild packs of dogs are reported to roam the countryside, causing disturbances in neighborhoods and in rural locations. Though wild in nature, they seem to have no fear of humans at all. They have even been seen digging in trashcans and empting dumpsters especially when local grocery stores throw out old bacon. But the werewolf girl of Talbot County is just a myth, right? Or has her spirit some how come back in its true animal form?

The Civil Rights Spirit

Thomas Brewer was born in Saco, Alabama, on November 11, 1894. This area of Pike County, just south of Montgomery, had long been a rural location, and many of the black families that took up residence here were that of sharecroppers and farmers. Thomas Brewer worked hard on his father's farm as a boy but also received his education through high school and college in Selma, Alabama. He later received his medical degree from Meharry College in Nashville.

Doctor Thomas Brewer moved to Columbus in 1920 and opened a practice at 1025 First Avenue. He had long been a major contributor to the rights of blacks during the civil rights movement and opened a chapter of the National Association for the Advancement of Colored People (NAACP) in Columbus to help advance the rights of blacks in Georgia. He made an effort to integrate local schools and to advance the funding of schools throughout Muscogee County. He even worked to integrate the South Commons Golf Course to benefit all races.

In 1944, a black resident of Muscogee County named Primus King made his way to the courthouse on the morning of July Fourth to cast his vote in the Democratic Party's primary election. Primus was met by police officers before he could cast his vote and was forcefully removed from the courthouse and denied reentry to cast his ballot. Once the situation was brought to the attention of Thomas Brewer, he rallied to raise money to help fund the two-year legal battle against the State of Georgia and its restrictions on black voters and civil rights.

Number 1025 First Avenue is the former office of Doctor Thomas Brewer.

During this time, Primus King received numerous death threats from groups like the Ku Klux Klan, as did Thomas Brewer. The process was long and time consuming, but Brewer poured all his efforts into his work and played a pivotal part in civil rights affairs in Columbus, and in 1945 and 1946, the Supreme Court ruled in favor of King. After gaining a substantial victory in the Primus King case, Brewer turned his attention to other affairs in the community that would once again stir the racial pot and cause trouble for the Doctor.

In 1951, Doctor Brewer developed a very successful campaign to hire black police officers in the city of Columbus, and shortly after, four black men were hired to patrol the neighborhoods located in downtown Columbus. Though successful, Brewer found himself in the middle of a political nightmare when city officials accused him of using his political attributes to deny a white man the position of city postmaster. Brewer denied the accusations and continued his efforts in being productive with all aspects of his chapter of the NAACP.

Thomas Brewer had gained a cunning nickname from his community. The people who worked with him called him "Chief," and it was not uncommon for lots of people to refer to him by this particular name. As the years passed, more and more racially motivated and political turmoil would play a huge part in the fight for African Americans all over the country, but in Alabama and Georgia, violence had progressed to a very high level, and most blacks in the American South were living in fear.

In 1955, Rosa Parks refused to give her seat to a white passenger on a city bus in Montgomery, Alabama, and was arrested. This sparked a radical position for blacks during the civil rights movement, and key civil rights figures, such as Doctor Martin Luther King and Ralph Abernathy, who took up Doctor King's position after his assassination, were plunged into violence while trying to take a political and humanitarian stand on their rights as people. Violence between blacks and radical hate groups had erupted all over the South, and the death tolls associated with lynching, murders, rape and other violent crimes toward blacks were piling up dramatically.

In the 1950s and '60s the subject of race, particularly in the South was a very controversial and heated debate. Organizations that were affiliated with, as well as groups that were in, the NAACP worked together to fight diligently to stop the racial oppression of the Jim Crow era. Though victims of severe punishment, profiling and hate, blacks in the American South would no longer lie down and roll over for a country that was to enforce them as part of the same human race as those of any other color. On the heels of the Montgomery bus boycott, the potential for rioting and violence became even more evident, and everyone living in the American South was on edge.

On February 18, 1956, Luico Flowers, who owned a clothing store, and Thomas Brewer, whose office was just above the clothing store, witnessed the arrest of a black man in front of their businesses. The man was arrested in a rather violent nature by white police officers for a petty offense. These types of arrests were very common during this time due to the unstable nature between blacks and whites. Though Luico Flowers made no effort to acknowledge the arrest, Thomas Brewer, on the other hand, was very upset by the altercation. He approached Flowers about a false report given that the man arrested was resisting arrest. Brewer's report of the arrest stated that the man did not resist, and therefore, the brutal nature by the arresting officers was not warranted. When Flowers denied the brutal nature of the arrest, Brewer became enraged, and a heated argument between the two men erupted in the street just in front of their businesses.

Thomas Brewer carried a pistol in his front pocket. With all the death threats he had received over the years and the promise of violence at anytime during the civil rights movement, he was extremely wary of any potential adversary. While the men argued, Flowers called the police because he feared that Brewer may harm him. Once the police arrived, the men continued their disagreement. Allegedly, Brewer reached in his pocket for his pistol and threatened to shoot Luico Flowers. Flowers then fired on Brewer and shot him seven times, claiming self-defense. Brewer was later pronounced dead at the scene, but a huge conspiracy erupted from the death of Brewer that remains a mystery to this day.

Brewer was a key figure in the community, especially among civil rights activists. Some speculate that his death was plain murder, but many people have disagreed and attested to the fact that though Brewer was not a violent man, he was prone to never back down from a fight. Flowers, a white man, was accompanied by two white policemen that fateful day in February, and many people still believe the murder was covered up by local authorities. So what really happened during that heated argument between Thomas Brewer and Luico Flowers? The evidence suggests that Brewer may not have even pulled his pistol since it was found inside his left pants pocket and had not been fired. This suggests he never pulled his gun on Flowers at all, and the question remains that if Brewer, who worked to fight against racial stereotypes, knew he was outnumbered by authorities and that his word was no match against that of a white man, why would he make such an irrational and bold decision to do so in front of men he knew would surely arrest him at the first inappropriate move or suggestion? The mystery still remains, and so does the spirit of Thomas Brewer. His office was located just below the Springer Opera House on First Avenue, and on occasion, people have reported seeing the spirit of Thomas Brewer here.

His office is a working establishment now, but the marker out front serves as a reminder of the tyranny and injustice that a whole race was to face during the civil rights movement. Some say that Doctor Brewer's ghost stays around to ensure that his goals and accomplishments are still making progress. Others suggest that he is still looking for justice for his alleged murder. The legends that came about after Brewer's death are few and far between, but it's known that Brewer may have received justice by way of haunting Flowers into his grave. Luico Flowers was charged but never arrested or convicted of the murder of Doctor Thomas Brewer. The Columbus grand jury would not indict Flowers since he pled that he shot Brewer in self-defense.

Flowers continued to work in his clothing store after the alleged murder, but shortly after the incident, he started to witness strange phenomenon. It's rumored that Flowers once closed his store in the middle of a work day after he felt the ghostly chill of a spirit haunting his establishment. He started to display unusual behavior and was nearly always paranoid. He claimed to hear voices while working in his store, and on occasion, he would see what he described as poltergeist activity. When he would leave the shop at night and return the following day, he would often find articles of clothing stacked in unusual patterns all over the store.

Though Flowers retained his innocence in the murder of Thomas Brewer for nearly a year, Flowers was found dead almost a year to the day of the death of Thomas Brewer. His death was ruled a suicide by a self-inflicted gunshot wound to the head. Did Thomas Brewer seek out his revenge on Luico Flowers by driving him to commit suicide? Today, people believe that the suicide of Flowers was, in a way, an admission of his guilt and that his involvement with the cover-up may have been what drove him to relieve himself of life.

Another rumor that started circulating in early 2007 suggests that many spirits of the civil rights era have found their way here to Columbus and now congregate in the location of Brewer's old office. One Columbus native reported that while she was walking in front of Doctor Brewer's old office, she heard men talking. When she looked over to acknowledge the conversation, she saw four black men and one black woman. She described the men as being very well dressed in suits and ties, but the clothes were very outdated. She described one man as being very tall and handsome and wearing black framed glasses. The others were dressed in similar suits, but one of the men bore a striking resemblance to Thomas Brewer, and the woman, she said, "Looked very much like a young, Coretta Scott King."

In the late 1970s, the wife of the late Doctor Marin Luther King did in fact visit the Fort Benning area in an effort to support the case of Carlton Gary, also known as the "Stocking Strangler." She met with local reporters to proclaim that a peaceful resolution should be found regarding the hostilities and tensions escalating in the area due the racial circumstances of the case.

Still, reports of Doctor Thomas Brewer's spirit circulate from time to time, and evidence exists that indicates the ghost of Thomas Brewer is still hanging around. Digital audio recorders have picked up a male voice near the 1000 block of First Avenue. When local paranormal investigators from the Alabama Paranormal Research Team stood outside the location and asked several questions, one answer was heard over the digital recorder. When an investigator asked, "Can you tell me your name?" a voice of an unknown entity answered, "Chief."

Malcolm X once stated, "We declare our right on this earth...to be a human being, to be respected as a human being, to be given the rights of a human being in this society, on this earth, in this day, which we intend to bring into existence by any means necessary." These words are uncanny and unadulterated and seem to resurrect the civil rights movement in the hearts of Americans today. It's possible that Thomas Brewer's spirit was so profound in his work that, even in death, he seeks to eradicate racial discrimination and to raise the oppressions placed on those of a different race, color or creed, a fearless champion of the rights of his people.

Haint Tales of Columbus Mills

Workhouses, mills and factories abandoned by time and forgotten by memory may be just the place for a wayward spirit to find some peace and quiet. Perhaps it's the solitude of abandonment or the memory of a place that keeps a ghost or two. Regardless, old factories house these spirits and keep the legends of many a Columbus ghost story.

The Eagle Phenix Phantom Fires

The Eagle Phenix Mill is located across the Chattahoochee River on the Georgia side in Columbus, just over the Horace King Friendship Bridge. This mill has long been a source of legend and more than a few ghostly fires. The Eagle Manufacturing Company was built in 1851, under the ownership of William H. Young. The factory was the second largest in Georgia, and material was made here for Confederate uniforms and other goods needed to help promote the Confederate cause.

When Union general James Wilson led his raid on the city of Columbus in April 1865, the Union forces set fire to the mill and burned it to the ground. They also confiscated the bell located in the tower at the time. The Mill was rebuilt in 1869 and renamed the Eagle Phenix Mill as a tribute to its rise from the ashes. The mill eventually became four times its original size and was the

The Eagle Phenix Mill is perhaps the most recognized feature on the Chattahoochee River in Columbus.

largest of its kind in the nation. The Eagle Phenix Mill manufactured over one hundred different varieties of cotton and wool products.

Over the years, the Eagle Phenix Mill has had several episodes with fire. Some were work related during its years of operation, but others have no origin. Over the years, while the building was vacant, fires were a constant problem, and the fire department was a regular guest at the old mill. Locals say that the phantom fires at the mill are a prelude to its name. Though the fires have long been associated with the mill, it has yet to meet its demise. In January 2000, a huge fire consumed much of the interior of the old factory and gutted many of the top floors. Although the fire started in the top floor, its cause could not be determined.

Today, the mill still stands as a testimonial to its name. Eagle Phenix apartments and condominiums now reside in the old mill and house many Columbus residences. These residents still report the phantom smells of burning wood inside the mill. People living in the Eagle Phenix apartment complex frequently report seeing smoke and flames in some areas of the building, and many of them frantically call neighbors along with local fire departments. Firefighters would arrive only to discover there was no smoke or fire. It seems irrational to think that a fire could actually haunt a building, but with the old mill still in a living state, it's appropriate that the company's name has branded a legacy onto the building's stone façade as the mystic fire continues to resurrect itself like the mystical firebird.

The One-Armed Girl at Johnston Mill Lofts

The Johnston Mill Lofts are located at 3201 First Avenue in Columbus. This part of the old mill complex was originally the Columbus Manufacturing Company and was part of the cotton warehouse that was used to store and later mill cotton. Once the mill incorporated the use of cotton gins in the early 1800s, productivity increased dramatically. Though child labor laws restricted children under the age of fifteen to work in a factor after 1836, some still found work in the mills; most lied about their age, as it was the easiest method in acquiring a mill job. Mill foremen were also not required to see any form of identification, so getting a good paying job in the mill was not difficult.

A legend has evolved from the early days of this mill about a young girl who had her hand severed in a mill accident. Rumor has it that a girl, roughly around the age of twelve, was working near a cotton gin when she managed to get part of her sleeve wedged in the hooks that were used to pull cotton away from the seed. She frantically tried to rip her clothing to separate herself from the machine but became trapped by the hooks. The machine pulled her arm in and mangled her arm, which later had to be amputated from the elbow down. She survived the accident but is said to still be making appearances more than 150 years later.

Today, the Columbus Manufacturing Company is dead, but the hustle and bustle of the Johnston Mill Lofts is now swarming with the living. Columbus State University students often rent the apartments since the location is close to campus and rent is cheap. However, one feature amenity, not included on the rental list, is the ghost of the one-armed girl. Renters are all too familiar with the story of the girl, who is seen most often in the stairwells of the building. Some have seen her in the hallways, and others report she takes up residence inside their apartments. A common thread of nearly all the Columbus mill stories is that the sound of working machinery is heard in the building late at night, as if the Columbus Manufacturing Company is still milling out cotton.

The spirit of this young girl may live on in the Johnston Mill Lofts because she is still working the old cotton gins, or it could be that she seeks the comfort of the living. Perhaps she finds some connection to those now living in her old work place. Whatever the reason, she is still there, and sightings of her apparition grow in number every year. Her work place may be long gone, but it's safe to say that she isn't going anywhere.

THE BIBB CITY MILL LIGHTS

Bibb City was considered a city inside a city and was an independent area of Muscogee County for several years. Bibb City was not incorporated into Columbus until 2000. The Bibb City Mill was the center of the location, and the mill village around it housed several hundred workers and their families. The Bibb City Cotton Mill was the largest cotton mill in the country at the height of its production period, employing more than two thousand workers.

The old mill in Bibb City was erected in 1900, on a part of the Chattahoochee River known as Lovers' Leap, and by 1920, construction started on the large building with its signature clock. In 1922, the structure was complete and an addition to the mill village was added and production flourished. In 1927, the mill became the largest cotton plant in America with 1,025 spindles, 300 looms, a warehouse space for 65,000 bales of cotton and 25,000 workers.

The mill hit a low point in the early 1930s during the Depression, but production rose to an all-time high during World War II. Later, Anderson Mill was acquired and incorporated into the mill complex, but by 1971, both mills had started to decline rapidly. The Bibb City Mill was dying out, and after several layoffs of hundreds of millers in March 1998, the Bibb City Mill closed its doors for good. But some did not leave. Ever since the mills closed, phantom lights have been seen inside the old building. Though it once had electricity to power its spindles and looms, the majority of the old long mill is gone. Only the front section with the handsome clock on top is left. Still, people see the lights go off and on inside the old structure.

Some speculate it is the work of the devil that keeps the lights on in the old mill. Early on the morning of October 31, 2008, a fire destroyed the structure on a massive scale, and most of the building was condemned. Though the source of the fire was undetermined by city and ATF officials,

The Bibb City Mill is no longer in service, but its hellfire mercenaries are faithfully lighting the way, enticing would-be victims to come in.

the lights inside the old mill are still seen. Much like its cousin, the Eagle Phenix Mill, it refuses to be destroyed, breathing a fiery spark occasionally to show the living that it and its ghostly millwrights are still hard at work.

The lights seen at the old Bibb Mill have been described in many aspects, but all generally revolve around the fact that whatever the building is still housing emanates a fiery glow. Based on the trademark fire in 2008, the building is not structurally sound and those brave enough to venture onto the premises on Halloween or venture inside would most likely find themselves in a dangerous situation. It's not recommended that you explore this location for threat of bodily injury (or far worse, if you're caught in a renegade fire.)

So exercise caution on those Halloween nights when you seek out your local haunts for a fright. The Bibb City Mill is no longer in service, but its hellfire mercenaries are faithfully lighting the way, enticing would-be victims to come in.

Ghostly Minstrels of Liberty Theatre

The Liberty Theatre is located on Eighth Avenue in Columbus, just a few blocks from the home of Gertrude "Ma" Rainey, who managed and preformed there regularly. The building has a colorful and vibrant history. Performers like Ella Fitzgerald, Al Green, Lena Horne, Duke Ellington and Fletcher Wilson are just a few of the souls to bless this theater with their presence and soulful music. The theater was built in 1924 and opened for business in 1925. It originally was a movie house, but the Liberty also had a stage for performances and plays.

The influence of music and theater in Columbus was a huge part of the cultural reflections during this era, and to have a theater that was owned and operated by African Americans was a critical foothold for blacks at the time. For fifty years, the Liberty Theatre played a pivotal role in the influence on culture in Columbus by bringing outstanding black performers to the area and enabling people to celebrate theater and music through dazzling performances and world famous performers.

The Liberty has withstood time and disrepair, and it is now totally renovated and serves as the Cultural Arts–African American Arts Institution and Musical Playhouse. Still a few ghostly specters are roaming this facility even in its renovated state. For years after the death of Ma Rainey, people reported her spirit being seen at the Liberty Theatre. Some reports from projectionist say that her full-figured silhouette could be seen from the projection booth, and the clanging sounds of gold bangles and shiny diamond rings would typically accompany this

The Liberty Theatre served Columbus for more than fifty years as the city's only African American theater and performance hall.

voluptuous, vaudeville spirit. However, when the source of the shadow was investigated, no one could be found.

Assuming the spirit of Ma Rainey is still at the Liberty Theatre, it would only seem fitting that other performers may still be performing a phantasmal play from time to time. Some of the oldest reports of these supernatural shows are that of an entire band that manifests on the performance stage and plays an entire ragtime jazz set. The performers are typically always reported to be wearing sophisticated 1930s attire and play everything from the saxophone and piano to the drums and double bass. The smell of cigarette and cigar smoke fills the air, and music flows from the great beyond into the hallowed halls of the old theater.

The spirits of the Liberty are never malevolent or mean and seem to not even acknowledge the people witnessing them. It's a little known fact that theater houses can essentially bring a supernatural energy to life through performances, song and dance. They have long been associated with religious and ritualistic concepts that song helps heal the soul. Music can breathe life into a body by stimulating the mind, and the ghostly performers at the Liberty Theatre seem to be continuing to do just that, bringing a life force into an inanimate object housing supernatural forces of a time period long forgotten. These soulful players will live on forever in this house of musical wonderment.

Muscogee County Tuberculosis Hospital

Tuberculosis, also called TB, is a disease caused by bacterium that infects lung tissue, causing severe upper respiratory infection and is typically fatal. The disease has not been eradicated globally, and several thousands of people, especially in third world countries, still die from it annually. In the United States, the casualty rate from tuberculosis is much lower, but a few cases still present every year. In the early 1900s, tuberculosis was a thriving epidemic and doctors all over the world strived to treat patients and figure out how to eradicate the highly contagious and deadly outbreaks of the disease.

As early as 1920, tuberculosis hospitals started popping up in every part of the United States. The treatment for the disease consisted of fresh air, good nutrition and adequate, around-the-clock medical care. The disease had to be treated acutely until a cure could be found, and at the height of the Great Depression, many tuberculosis hospitals found themselves struggling to handle the growing number of TB patients.

Perhaps the most noted tuberculosis hospital and notoriously haunted facility can be found in Louisville, Kentucky. The Waverly Hills Sanatorium was a self-sufficient tuberculosis hospital capable of caring for hundreds of patients. However, it was also a facility that participated in experimental medicine. Experiments were conducted on patients by doctors in an effort to find a way to treat or replace damaged and infected lung tissue. Some patients underwent lobectomy, which is a procedure to remove the infected lungs. Occasionally, doctors would replace the entire lung with balloons that were designed to mimic lung function; others underwent thoracoplasty, which was the removal of as many as seven to eight ribs. This procedure allowed the lungs to collapse and ease the strain of air flow. Typically, several operations were performed, removing two and three ribs during one procedure.

Though many of these experimental procedures were a failure, some patients did live for days and sometimes weeks under painful circumstances before dying, despite the efforts to save them. Essentially, tuberculosis would render itself as a leading killer among people during the early and mid-1900s. Patients with tuberculosis were spread out all over the United States in many hospitals. Some of the most notable tuberculosis hospitals of early nineteenth-century Georgia include Battey State Hospital, which was turned into a TB hospital in 1946 and is located in Rome, Georgia. The hospital treated nearly two thousand patients. Another was Fairhaven Hospital in Athens, Georgia, constructed in 1926 and treating TB patients from the 1930s to the 1940s. Lee Arrendale State Prison in Alto, Georgia, was originally built as a hospital in 1926 and also treated tuberculosis patients until the mid-1950s. And then there's Muscogee County Tuberculosis Hospital in Columbus, which was built in 1938. The structure housed nearly one hundred patients and had an octagon shaped copula surrounded by windows located in the center of the facility. The structure was designed to allow fresh air to flow into all parts of the building.

Though no records exist of any experimental treatment of patients at the Muscogee County Tuberculosis Hospital, it is speculated that all TB facilities were involved in the same efforts as Waverly Hills Sanatorium as part of a collaborated effort to eradicate the disease. Prior to 1962, the hospital was closed, and the Junior League of Women operated the facility as a nursing home. They remodeled and renamed the facility "Highland House," and it was the first nursing home facility in Columbus. The Highland House operated as a nursing home until the mid-1990s, when it was closed and a new facility was built to house the ever-growing population of elderly patients.

Today, the building is used as a maintenance facility, but lawn mowers and tool sheds are not the only things lingering in the old hospital nursing home. As early as the 1960s, stories about supernatural activity have circulated within nursing staff and patients alike. Ghostly apparitions have been seen manifesting in hallways and wandering the corridors of the old building. According to nursing staff, on a spring afternoon in May 1965, a nurse from Columbus named Margaret entered the room of an elderly gentleman to check on him and administer his medications. The man was nearly eighty

The Muscogee County Tuberculosis Hospital was built in 1938. The facility was dedicated to the treatment of patients with tuberculosis, but death was all too common here.

years old but was in a rather good mental state, according to Margaret. When she entered his room, he appeared to be talking to someone, though no one else was there. Margaret asked him who he was talking to, and he answered that the gentleman from the next room had been visiting with him all day. Margaret was a bit confused since the gentleman who was in the next room was bedridden and immobile.

Margaret feared her elderly patient might be suffering from dementia, so she noted his odd behavior in his chart and left the room. As Margaret left her patient's room, her curiosity spiked, and she decided to go to the neighboring room where the bedridden man was. She knocked just slightly on the door as she entered and found the fragile man lying soundly in his bed. She checked his vital signs and started for the curtains to allow some more light into the room. She was then met by the ghostly apparition of a man in a hospital gown. Margaret had not seen him standing there a second ago, and she stood looking at the man for several seconds. Finally, the man reached out for her and then vanished. Margaret let out a deafening scream, so loud that she woke her patient and hospital staff came running to her aid. She was completely terrified by what she had just seen.

She knew the man wasn't a patient of hers or any of the other nurses' in the home, and she would not be the last to see him. On another occasion, a different nurse was tending to a patient in the same area of the Highland House and came across a man standing in the hallway, peering into a patient's room. She looked down the hallway at the man and did not notice him as one of her patients. She thought he might have wandered over from another wing, so she walked down the hallway in his direction. "Sir, Sir!" she shouted, but he did not acknowledge her. As she approached him, she could see he was barefoot and looked rather pale. He, too, was wearing a hospital gown, and when she reached to take hold of his arm, she noticed his skin was as cold as ice. She looked up at his face, and what she saw shook her to the very core. The man's face was white, and his eye sockets were offset by the sunken tissue around his check bones. He had no eyes! Just dark hollow sockets filled with blackness.

This event haunted this particular nurse for most of her life, and the story has been passed down for generations in her family. No one knows who the man is that haunts the hollow halls of the old tuberculosis hospital in Columbus, but manifestations of his spirit can be felt on the property as well. Visitors who have come to the old building report feeling ice cold breezes even on the hottest summer days in the front corridors, both in and outside of the building. A story has developed that this eyeless spirit is simply a wayward soul, waiting to be cured of the dreadful disease that perhaps took his life. Or maybe he wanders the hallways, seeking an after-life companion. It's a sad existence to say the least, being trapped in a place that attempted to find a cure but later housed the elderly and dying. It's the physical manifestation of death even in the realm of the living.

BIBLIOGRAPHY

PRINT

Adams, Jasmin Interview by author. Waverly Hall. May 1, 2012

Adams, P.J. Interview by author. Waverly Hall, GA. May 1, 2012

Cathey, Joyce. Interview by author. Ellerslie, GA. September 2012

Cathey, Joyce S., and Rebecca S. Harrington. *The Veil: Heidi Wyrick's Story*. Lincoln, NE: iUniverse 2007.

Cherry, Francis Lafayette. *The History of Opelika and Her Agricultural Tributary Territory*. Opelika, AL: Genealogical Society of East Alabama, 1996.

Cobis, Monica. Interview by author. Columbus, GA, Date. April, 2012

Columbus Ledger Enquirer.

Ingram, Susan. Interview by author. Columbus, GA, January 2011.

Kennedy, Linda J. and Mary Jane Galer. *Historic Linwood Cemetery*. Charleston, SC: Arcadia Publishing, 2004.

O'Connell, Deirdre. *The Ballad of Blind Tom, Slave Pianist: America's Lost Musical Genius*. New York: Overlook Publishers, 2009.

Pierce, Paul. *The Springer Ghost Book: A Theatre Haunting in the Deep South.* Columbus, Georgia: Communicorp, 2003.

Thomas, Kenneth H., Jr. *Fort Benning*. Charleston, SC: Arcadia Publishing, 2003.

Wyrick, Lisa. Interview by author. Ellerslie, GA, Date. September 2012

WEBSITES

Ancestry.com. Accessed May 2012. www.ancestry.com.

Muscogee Manor and Rehabilitation Center. Last Modified September 2010. Accessed April 2012. www.muscogeemanorga.com.

About the Author

Faith Serafin is a historian and folklorist from Lee County, Alabama. She is a volunteer at Port Columbus-National Civil War Naval Museum and an official tour guide of the Sea Ghosts Tours. She is also the director of the Alabama Paranormal Research Team, which was organized in 2007 and which aims to seek out the paranormal aspects as it pertains to historical locations. She dedicates much of her time to the preservation of history and education. Faith also works with local schools to help promote reading fundamentals and the importance of community history through education. Faith has one previous publication and several short, historical legend and folklore stories published online. Many of Faith's published information regarding historical and haunted locations, tours and events can be found on her website: www.AlabamaGhostHunters.com.